The Theology of
St. John

JOSEPH CREHAN, S.J.

SHEED AND WARD · NEW YORK

TO THE NEWMAN ASSOCIATION
IN MEMORY OF PORTMAN SQUARE

Contents

Preface

The last ten years have seen the appearance of three large commentaries on St. John: by Professor C. H. Dodd (Congregationalist), by Professor C. K. Barrett (Methodist) and by the late R. H. Lightfoot (Anglican). Catholic output has been by contrast meagre, but, by way of compensation, there is a most valuable study of the interpretation of the fourth gospel among the Fathers of the early and undivided Church, published by the Rev. M. F. Wiles of Cambridge under the title *The Spiritual Gospel* (Cambridge, 1960). Here the comments of Origen, Cyril of Alexandria or Theodore of Mopsuestia are made accessible to the Greekless reader most liberally. Overshadowing all this recent work is the great book of Sir Edwin Hoskyns *The fourth gospel* (here cited from the second edition of 1947, by author's name and page number alone). Its influence has been widespread in France as well as at home, though not to any great extent in Germany. What has become apparent as a trend in recent work is the cautious return to acceptance of the possibility that, after all, the gospel may have been written by the apostle himself. The Bishop of Woolwich, writing in *The gospels reconsidered* (Oxford, 1960), admits that the conservative position about this authorship (which was defended by Bishops Westcott and Lightfoot in the past) "continues to have protagonists who are no fools", and he cites four names: A. C. Headlam, *The fourth gospel as history* (1948); A. H. Green-Armytage, *John who saw* (1952); H. E. Edwards, *The Disciple who wrote these things* (1953) and R. A. Edwards, *The Gospel*

according to St. John (1954). He also makes the point that both the witness and the theology of the fourth gospel are remarkably primitive. In view of contemporary German attempts to interpret John with the help of the philosophy of Heidegger, this admission is of great importance. At least, one may go forward with a working hypothesis that the apostle was responsible for both gospel and letters, even if one is not ready to share the viewpoint of the present writer that it was in fact the apostle who wrote them. For the further question of the identity of authorship of gospel and Apocalypse, the work of Fr. Martindale, both in his discussion of the Apocalypse in the *Catholic Commentary on Scripture* (Edinburgh, 1953) and in his schoolbook on the gospel (London, 1956) may be referred to, for it states all that is essential.

The publication of two Bodmer papyri of St. John (which are here cited under their official designations as P 66 and P 75) has naturally stimulated discussions of the text of the fourth gospel. Both are in book form and not in scroll form, and one of the two has numbered pages. This, fact along with the early date of the papyrus (about 180–210), makes it very unlikely that transpositions of the text of the gospel took place at an early stage of its transmission. The only hope of modern editors who wish to suppose that there were transpositions is to be able to prove that John wrote on unnumbered loose sheets of papyrus, that he died immediately after completing his gospel and that his disciples gathered the sheets in the wrong order. Probability is against each of these three hypotheses taken by itself and their joint fulfilment would be nothing short of marvellous.

It is recorded of St. Cuthbert (by John of Salisbury)

that he was wont to cure the sick by placing on them a copy of the gospel of St. John, and his own copy (the one now preserved at Stonyhurst) was placed under his head when he was buried. The devotion of Edward the Confessor to St. John is well-known, and it is pleasant to think that the English Province of the Society of Jesus showed its desire to continue this devotion by dedicating to him the first permanent house it possessed (at Louvain), and later on by the care it took of the Anglo-Saxon copy of his gospel already referred to, when once it returned to Catholic hands. If the present work helps to continue that devotion, it will have achieved its purpose.

27 *December* 1963

Bibliography

THE principal commentaries in English, C. K. Barrett *The Gospel according to St. John* (1955), Sir E. Hoskyns, *The fourth gospel* (2nd edn., 1947) and C. H. Dodd, *The Interpretation of the fourth gospel* (1953) are all cited simply by the name of the author and the page. Professor Dodd's second Johannine work *Historical tradition in the fourth gospel* (1963) appeared when this work was already in typescript and has been used only in one or two places. The usual abbreviations are used for the books of Old and New Testaments. References to the gospel of John are given by chapter and verse-number alone, without the repetition of the word *John* each time. The Qumran documents are cited from T. H. Gaster's *Scriptures of the Dead Sea Sect* (1957) and the Talmud from the Soncino edition. The Bodmer papyri of St. John were edited by V. Martin, *Bodmer Papyrus* II (1956), with supplement (1958), and *Bodmer Papyrus* XV (1961).

OTHER WORKS CONSULTED INCLUDE:

L. Alonso-Schökel, *Estudios de Poetica Hebrea* (1963);
J. H. Bernard, *The Gospel according to St. John* (2 vols., 1928);
F. M. Braun, *Jean le théologien et son évangile* (1959);
R. Bultmann, *Das Evangelium des Johannes* (latest edn., 1957);
C. F. Burney, *The Aramaic Origins of the fourth gospel* (1922);
the same, *The poetry of Our Lord* (1925);

9

E. Burrows, 'The Doctrine of the Shekinah' (in *Gospel of the Infancy and other essays,* 1940);

Y. Congar, *The Mystery of the Temple* (1962);

F. L. Cross (editor), *The Gospels reconsidered* (1960);

C. H. Dodd, *According to the Scriptures* (1952);

J. Donovan, *The authorship of the fourth gospel* (1935);

R. A. Edwards, *The Gospel according to St. John* (1954);

P. Gächter, articles in *Zeitschrift für katholische Theologie* (1934), (1935) and (1936);

B. Gärtner, *John 6 and the Jewish Passover* (1959);

R. M. Grant, *Historical introduction to the New Testament* (1963);

A. Green Armytage, *John who saw* (1952);

A. C. Headlam, *The fourth gospel as history* (1948);

A. Guilding, *The fourth gospel and Jewish worship* (1960);

R. H. Lightfoot, *St. John's gospel: a commentary* (1956);

T. W. Manson, *Studies in the gospels and epistles* (1962);

C. R. North, *The suffering servant* (2nd edn., 1956);

J. N. Sanders, *The fourth gospel in the early Church* (1943);

A. Wainwright, *The Trinity in the New Testament* (1962);

M. F. Wiles, *The spiritual gospel* (1960).

AMERICAN EDITION OF WORKS QUOTED:

C. K. Barrett, *The Gospel according to St. John* (New York, Seabury, 1955).

C. H. Dodd, *The Interpretation of the Fourth Gospel* (New York, Cambridge U. Press, 1953) and *Historical Tradition in the Fourth Gospel* (New York, Cambridge U. Press, 1963).

T. H. Gaster, ed., *The Dead Sea Scriptures* (New York, Doubleday, 1956).

E. Hoskyns, *The Fourth Gospel* (Naperville, Ill., Allenson, 1947).

A. Wainwright, *The Trinity in the New Testament* (Naperville, Ill., Allenson, 1962).

I

The Johannine Writings

THE *corpus* of the writings of John, gospel, Apocalypse and three Epistles, does not seem to have been collected separately in antiquity as the Pauline *corpus* was. One of the Bodmer papyri (P 75) has the gospel of John together with that of Luke on some thirty-six folded sheets of papyrus while the other Bodmer papyrus (P 66) seems to have contained John's gospel by itself. The Apocalypse, though it was stoutly championed by Papias early in the second century (or perhaps because of this), was regarded by many Eastern bishops as being of questionable canonicity and did not find a place in their bibles at all. The First Epistle may have been a "covering letter" to go out with the gospel to some church that had asked for a copy, though its language shows in places some development beyond the point reached in the gospel. The Second and Third Epistles are simple occasional pieces and cannot be supposed to represent the whole of John's correspondence. If their survival had been due to a desire to save all that he ever wrote, one would have expected them to have many companion-pieces. It may be that these two survived in the church which had witnessed the machinations of Diotrephes, where they were needed as a guarantee that such moves would not be repeated. The seven letters to the churches which comprise the factual part of the Apocalypse (as distinct from the visionary part) were never combined with these Second and Third Epistles to form a book of Johannine letters.

The arguments from internal evidence for a difference of authors of Apocalypse and gospel do not carry conviction. It is more obvious to the present age than it was a generation ago that the same man can write in two quite different styles. There are now many scientists or medical experts who try their hands at the writing of detective stories, often under assumed names, though in the past generation the solitary examples of Stephen Leacock and Professor Cole may not have seemed sufficient justification for a generalization. The subject-matter of the Apocalypse, with all its reminiscences of Ezechiel, Zacharias and Isaias, and its traditional laws of symbolism, is quite adequate as an explanation of the fact that a word-count shows some divergence between the vocabulary of the gospel and that of the Apocalypse. On the other hand, certain key-words, such as the word *Logos*, are common to both, and also certain tricks of language. It used to be commonly held that a span of some ten years separated the two works, the gospel coming at the end of the century and the Apocalypse at some time before that, during the persecution of Domitian (who was assassinated in 96). Today there are those (e.g. Professor Robert Grant) who would date the gospel as early as 70, since they see in it points of contact with the Dead Sea scrolls and think that the existence of so much second century papyrus-evidence for the circulation of the gospel warrants the moving back of its date of composition, but this reversal of order between the two works does not seem quite satisfactory.

The vision of Apoc 14:6 is of an angel "flying in mid-heaven, carrying with him a final gospel to preach to all those who dwell on the earth" (so the Knox version), but in the Chester Beatty papyrus and in *codex Sinaiticus*

there is an important variant reading which has all the appearance of being the original. The verb is there put down as aorist middle and not active, so that the sense is not that the angel himself preaches the gospel once for all, but that he *gets it done* once for all. This might be a glimpse of the once-for-all canonization of the fourfold gospel, whether that event be regarded as already past or still to come. The part played by John in this formation of the gospel-*corpus* has been discussed at some length by the present author [in Essay III of *The gospels reconsidered* (1960)], and perhaps a reference to that work may be found helpful at this point.

The vision of the Tetramorph (Apoc 4:6–7) does not necessarily mean that the gospel of John was already completed at the time of this vision. It would be sufficient to suppose that the vision gave a warrant for the gathering of the gospels together and their completion by the addition of a fourth to the existing three. One may note in passing that the earliest interpretation of this vision, found in Irenaeus and in Victorinus of Pettau (who had, both in independence of each other, made use of Papias), is to equate John with the lion and Mark with the eagle. The order of the figures in the vision of Ezechiel is: man, lion, calf, eagle. It may be that the change of order here was thought of by John as significant, the lion being put first to indicate what he was expected to do by way of completing the gospel. With a Jewish love of patterning the wicked beast of Apoc 13:1–3 is seen as another Tetramorph, having the shape of a pard, the feet of a bear, the mouth of a lion and being endued with the power of the dragon.

Jewish love of patterning is manifest throughout the Apocalypse, but it is not entirely absent from the gospel.

One does not find in the gospel a clearly marked five-fold division such as is presented in the gospel of Matthew, but there are signs of what Papias would have called *taxis* (or patterning) about its composition. There is a refrain that keeps cropping out from time to time to the effect that all this was not understood at the time but was made clear later on, after the Resurrection. One can find this at Jn 2:22; 7:39; 12:16; 13:7; 14:26 and 16:4. A recent writer has seen attempts at conscious parallelism between the events of Jn 6 (the multiplication of loaves and the sea scene) and those of Jn 21, and if this latter chapter is an epilogue put in as an after-thought, there may have been such a conscious effort to provide reminiscences of the earlier chapter. One has to be careful about noticing parallels, however, for some investigators of the Apocalypse, through too much concentration on their task, seem to contract a disease that impairs their critical faculty, very much as those who work for long periods submerged in pressure-chambers under the sea are liable to the disease that is popularly called "the bends".

No one can deny that the Apocalypse is dominated by groupings of sevens, however much the details may be open to dispute. Nothing like this can be found in the gospel, since after all there was a factual thread to be followed in that work, but modern writers such as Cullmann have been anxious to find in the gospel a sacramental schematism based on the theology of its author. This should not be pressed, but it may well be that, at the time of writing of the gospel, interest in the liturgical life of the Church required that greater attention to its origins be given than was thought necessary by the earlier evangelists. Later chapters here will show how the themes of Life and Light run through the gos-

pel, and each of these is illustrated by a miracle that is described at length, the man born blind in Jn 9 and the restoring to life of Lazarus in Jn 11. These two miracles are linked (by Jn 11:37 and 12:9; 12:17) with the events of the Passion, thus suggesting that the offer of Life and Light, followed by the rejection of that offer, is as familiar to the author as it was to Matthew who fashioned his gospel as a story of rejection.

There are no OT Scripture quotations in the three Epistles, though Cain is once adduced as an example. In the gospel the manner in which the OT is used suggests that the author is somewhat independent in his rendering of the Hebrew, as he does not seem to follow any known Greek version. On the other hand his mind is full of parallelisms; he cannot keep himself from putting down in his Epistles sayings such as the one about the darkness already passing away and the light beginning to appear, and these betray a mind that thought in Hebrew and perhaps prayed thus, though whether that prayer was public or private one could not venture to say. This habit of an old man in his letters may throw some light on the question of the poetic form that some have detected in the discourses which are set down in the gospel. C. F. Burney first of all, and then P. Gächter following him, sought to establish a verse-structure for such discourses as that after the Last Supper or the one given at the synagogue of Capharnaum, with rhythmic stresses balancing the clauses as in a psalm of the OT. If this practice can be found in the Epistles, where no direct claim is made to be quoting the words of Christ, it would seem more likely that it was the author of the gospel and not Christ Himself who cast the gospel discourses into that form. The Synoptics do not generally lend themselves to such poetic analysis when they are

reporting discourses, though the *Pater* in Matthew's version could be so treated. One may think, then, of an old man who has spent a lifetime polishing these discourses until their poetic form satisfied him, but this would not mean that he altered their original content.

The apparent citation of Jn 6:51 in the Epistle of Barnabas: "Fair trees grow on the banks of the stream, and whoso shall eat of them shall live for eternity" (11:10) is probably to be explained (if one takes that Epistle as belonging to the decade 80–90) by supposing that some of the discourses which John was ultimately to write down for his gospel were already known from his oral teaching and had imprinted themselves on the memory of another who could not easily forget their rhythm. The Bread of the Eucharist may easily have been envisaged as the fruit of the Tree of Life that grew by the waters of baptism, and the borrowing of a saying of Jesus that was already known from John's oral teaching would then be quite a simple proceeding. Other borrowings in the *Odes of Solomon* are less certain but, if established, could be explained on the same lines. It has even been argued recently by a Swedish scholar that the whole of the eucharistic discourse of Jn 6 was in use in the liturgy long before the whole gospel was written.

II

The Life of John

THE colophon of the fourth gospel (Jn 21:24–25) states clearly that the work has been written by the Beloved Disciple. It comes at the end of the episode of the prophecy about the way in which the Beloved Disciple was to end his life. Then follow the words: "This is the disciple who beareth witness concerning these things, and who hath written these things and we know that his witness is true." Naturally there has been much speculation about the identity of those who vouch for the gospel by adding the words: "We know that his witness is true", but several factors have in recent years combined to make an answer more easy. First of all, it is now impossible to suppose that these two verses are a later addition to the gospel, for the *Codex Sinaiticus*, when it was examined under ultra-violet light (after coming into the possession of the British Museum in 1932), showed that the scribe had originally made an omission here but went back and washed out what he had written to make a fresh start and give the whole text. Then the brilliant intuition of Sir E. Hoskyns (pp. 559–60) supplied an explanation of the sudden change from "this is" to "we know" by showing that the witness of the apostles was collective and that John as the last of them could very well have spoken for himself ("This is that disciple") and then added that all the Twelve vouched for what he said because from the beginning on the day of Pentecost they had been giving a combined or collegiate witness to the facts about Christ, being

acutely conscious that they were indeed Christ's witnesses (Lk 24:48). Hoskyns was making no wild conjecture, for in the body of the gospel there are signs of
such an idea of collective behaviour of the Twelve.
Thomas (in Jn 14:5) is made to ask: "How can we
know the way?", as if he spoke for them all, while in Jn
3:2 and 3:11 there is the same switch from singular to
plural in the words of Christ to Nicodemus: "I say unto
thee; we speak what we know . . ." Dodd wrote of this
verse: "It is at first sight tempting to remove 3:11 as an
editorial comment. But this temptation is to be resisted
. . . The testimony of 3:11 is that of Christ, but, as
occasionally elsewhere, the evangelist betrays the fact
that it is mediated corporately by the Church." (p. 328,
note 3.)

That the elders of Ephesus should have added a colophon to the gospel would be strange, in view of the fact
that no similar colophon exists in any other part of the
NT. We have to wait until the *Codex Alexandrinus* of the
early fifth century to find even such additions as those
made to the Epistles of St. Paul to indicate where he
was when he wrote them (in the form: It was written
from Corinth, etc.). The burden is entirely on the
exponents of such an hypothesis to show that such a
custom was ever known in classical literature, and this
they have not done. The fourth gospel went into circulation quickly, for the fragment at Manchester (Rylands papyrus 457) dates from somewhere about 120–
130 A.D. and might even be earlier. It was found in a
village of Middle Egypt, and though it was probably
not copied out there, the arrival of the gospel in Alexandria must have been somewhat prior to the decade
120–130; it would be very surprising if the very first
copy to reach Egypt had been the prototype from

which our Rylands papyrus was copied. The Rylands papyrus is itself a single sheet, too small to indicate what the work from which it was torn looked like, but the Bodmer papyrus of John (P 66, from the end of the second century) has numbered pages, and this seems to rule out the idea that tampering with the text could have gone on even at an earlier stage, for if the pages of such book-form papyri were numbered, interpolation becomes very difficult to envisage.

The traditional identification of John with the Beloved Disciple is already familiar to Polycrates of Ephesus, who was bishop there about 190, when he wrote to Pope Victor as follows: "In our church of Asia great pillars have been laid to rest; Philip in Hierapolis . . . and his daughter at Ephesus, and still more, John, he who leaned upon the Lord's breast, who had been a priest wearing the *petalos*, and was witness and teacher . . . He sleeps in Ephesus . . ." (Eusebius, HE 5:24). When Polycrates wrote this letter he was sixty-five, as he himself says; he was one of a family of bishops and had gathered his traditions from his forebears. One may therefore carry his evidence back to a date around 130, if not earlier. It is hard to think that local tradition of so short a span could have become seriously garbled.

The same tradition is present in the *Acts of John* (89), a tendentious composition from the middle of the second century, but one which had to aim at some verisimilitude in its narrative of events. It is also present in the reminiscences of Irenaeus. In the passage of his *adversus haereses* (3:1) where he sets out the gospels in what he conceived to be their order, John is characterized as the one who rested his head on the breast of Christ and who published (or gave out) his gospel while

he dwelt at Ephesus. Elsewhere (in the letter to Florinus, cited by Eusebius, HE 5:20) Irenaeus tells of his early contacts with Polycarp and of that great man's stories about his association with John and with others who had seen the Lord. As if to disarm criticism of his evidence, he points out that he is now old and can therefore remember the events of long ago much more clearly than what happened in the interim, a trait that has been noticed in other elderly folk. Irenaeus also says (*adv. haer.* 3:3:4) that Polycarp was baptized by apostles, and as from Polycarp's own statement this baptism took place about the year 70 (he died in 155, having served Christ for eighty-six years), one may infer that Polycarp had plenty of time to acquaint himself with John,[1] supposing that that Apostle lived until the time of Trajan (i.e. at least until 98 A.D.).

In the days of Modernism Baron von Hügel could attempt to whittle away the evidence of Irenaeus on the ground that he was, "at the most fifteen when frequenting Polycarp" (this did not take account of Irenaeus' remark that he remembered things from that time much better than the events of his later life), and that he had been mistaken in saying that Papias was "a hearer of John", meaning the Apostle, when in fact Papias was a disciple of the other John, called the Presbyter. Having been mistaken over Papias, argued von Hügel, Irenaeus could easily have been mistaken about Polycarp in the same way. It is difficult to see how Irenaeus could have misunderstood Polycarp when he claimed to have been baptized "by Apostles" (the plural might be boastful, but at least the presence of the longest-lived Apostle at

[1] Polycarp, as Lightfoot noted, uses expressions "characteristic of the Asiatic school of St. John" in his own brief Epistle to the Philippians.

his baptism seems certain). Von Hügel's case thus depends entirely on the supposed existence of a second John, the Presbyter, whom he is bold enough to call "the very real and important presbyter". But in fact this man is a creation of the imagination of Eusebius and he must now be discussed.

Eusebius was not enamoured of the Apocalypse; in HE 7:25 he cites a long attack on it by Denis of Alexandria, who had suggested that it was by another John, not the Apostle. This seemed an easy way out of the problem, and was moreover the way taken by Eusebius over another difficulty in Scripture. He had ventured to suppose that, when St. Paul "withstood Cephas to his face at Antioch", this was some other Cephas and not St. Peter. No one has followed him in this, but in his escape from the Johannine problem he has found more followers. That is perhaps because he gave as his reason an ambiguous passage from Papias (cited in HE 3:39) which must now be examined.

What Papias wrote may be translated as follows:

> If perchance at any time there came my way someone who had actually travelled about with the ancients, I would make enquiries about the sayings of the ancients—what did Andrew say? or Peter? what did Philip, or Thomas, or James say? what said John, or Matthew, or some other of the Lord's disciples?—and about what Aristion and the ancient, John, disciples of the Lord, were still saying. For I took it for granted that excerpts from the Books were not so helpful to me as the utterances of the living voice of a survivor.

In this passage Papias is using the term "ancient" in the non-technical sense of "a man from before my time". He would have counted the apostles as ancients in this sense, and he shows that he had a healthy interest

in their sayings, whenever he could hear of them. He was probably a Jew (for there is at least one Rabbi Papias in the Talmud) and oral tradition was his delight. Most of the apostles were dead when he was of an age to collect their sayings intelligently, but there was one survivor, John, who had been absent from Asia and his active life of teaching for a period while he was a prisoner on Patmos, but who once more became available for questioning by disciples at Ephesus in his old age, after Domitian was dead and his prisoners had been amnestied. This return of John would account for his being mentioned twice in the list. There is no need to follow Eusebius in thinking that this second mention of the name denotes a second John. His companion, Aristion, is quite unknown, though it is a curious fact that the excavators at Ephesus have turned up the gravestone of a Tiberius Claudius Aristion. From his first two names this man must have lived in the first century A.D., and, though there is no evidence that he was a Christian, one can at least be sure that there were Aristions at Ephesus. One of these could have been in the party that wanted to speak with Jesus (Jn 12:21) at the final Pasch. The gospel certainly seems to go out of its way to name other figures who were known in Asia Minor, such as Andrew and Philip, in various episodes, and it might be that Aristion had his own niche in the narrative. This is no more than a conjecture, but it would fit all the facts so far as they are known. Papias shows a preference for oral tradition[1] over "excerpts from the Books" (i.e. the OT), and it is now quite common ground among critics that there were such

[1] Dodd (*Historical Tradition in the Fourth Gospel*, p. 305) rightly underlines the fact that the apostles named first in Papias's list are those known in Asia.

collections of important passages from the OT in circulation among Christians at the end of the first century.

When Tertullian (*de praescriptione haer.* 36) wanted to boast about the Christian glories of Rome, he said that it was the scene of John the Apostle being plunged into flaming oil and coming out unscathed. Now the account of the Neronian persecution given by Tacitus (*Annals* 15:44) says that some of them were punished, "by being burnt to death, so that when daylight waned they might be consumed to provide illumination for the night" (*Ut interirent . . . flammandi, atque ubi defecisset dies in usum nocturni luminis urerentur*). If one envisages this torture as the placing of the victims in large oil-jars which were then ignited, the result would be what Tacitus supposes in his account, while that of Tertullian would be near enough to provide a notable degree of corroboration. What would happen to John, if he did in fact escape from or survive this ordeal? One might conjecture that he was either sent into exile at Patmos now (and stayed there thirty years) or that he was spirited away by friends when he came unhurt from the fire and lay low in Asia Minor for some time, being able to baptize Polycarp there about six years later. His arrest and condemnation to exile in Patmos would then come at some time after 81 A.D., under Domitian.

III

The Idea of Witnessing in John

T HE idea of witnessing on the part of God was familiar to those who had read the Servant passages of Isaias (Isai 43:9-10)

Were all the nations gathered together, and the peoples assembled, who amongst them could declare these things? (i.e. what God of theirs could)

And these former things let them announce to us, let them produce their witnesses, that they may be justified, that the nations may hear and say: It is true.

> Ye are My witnesses, said Jahwe,
> and My servant whom I have chosen;
> that ye may know and believe Me,
> and understand that I am He.

The Exodus was one of the "former things" that Israel could point to as a witnessing by Jahwe to His own godhead in the eyes of the nations. Then Israel was the Servant, a collective personality, but when Jahwe shall once more witness in the future, will it be so again? There will be a future witness (Isai 43:13):

> I am God from eternity:
> And from today I am the same,
> and there is none that can deliver out of My hand;
> I will perform, and who can prevent it?

One may recognize at once that this passage must have been familiar to John who uses it at Jn 10:29; 13:3. Isaias goes on to show that the signs of Jahwe's new

witness will be the downfall of Babylon, the second Exodus and an outpouring of water and the Spirit (Isai 43:14 to 44:5). One can begin to see that already there is emerging a pattern according to which John might start to organize his material. The conversation of Moses and Elias with Christ at the Transfiguration was about His Exodus, as Luke reports; the fall of Babylon will be a large part of the theme of the Apocalypse, and the outpouring of water and Spirit appears as the theme of Jn 3 and 7. The wording of Isai 43:10 suggests that there will be a collective witness by a group and one by the chosen Servant as well. The result of witnessing is to be a faith "that I am He", an acceptance of the *Ego eimi* sayings which are studded throughout this gospel.

In Deut 19:15 the law of witnessing against a malefactor is laid down: "In the mouth of two witnesses and in the mouth of three the whole matter shall be established." Mk 14:55–56 says of the two witnesses against Our Lord at His trial that their testimony was not equal, i.e. that it did not correspond point for point. The story of Susanna gives another instance of this inequality of testimony. The collective witness of the apostles is more than enough to satisfy the condition of plurality, but it must appear to be "equal". How does John show this?

There are two planes of witnessing: "If we accept the witnessing of men, the witnessing of God is greater, and the witnessing of God is this, that He has rendered testimony about His Son" (1 Jn 5:9). On the human plane, the apostles show signs that they are aware of their job as witnesses. The Synoptics report generally the saying (Mt 10:18; Mk 13:9; Lk 21:13) that the disciples will be brought before the Sanhedrin, will be scourged in synagogues, will be cited before provincial governors and

emperors, and all as a witness against THEM AND THE
GENTILES. The hostile note is softened by Luke's edit-
ing, for he records simply: "It will turn out for you an
occasion of witnessing." John himself (Apoc 1:9) claims
that he was in Patmos on account of his witnessing to
Jesus. Above all there is his passage about the two witnesses (Apoc 11:3–12). Some of their features are those
of Elias and Moses; for instance, the closing of the
heavens to rain and the turning of water to blood, but
others are clearly reminiscent of Peter and Paul. The
fact that Peter was buried near the site of his martyrdom
is perhaps alluded to in 11:8–9; the city called spiritual
Sodom and Egypt is by general agreement Rome.

This Johannine language is not without parallel in
the rest of the NT. The apostles (Ac 4:33; 1:22) are
witnesses of the Resurrection, Peter describes himself as
a witness of the Passion of Christ (1 Pet 5:1) and as a
partaker of the Transfiguration. Paul (Ac 22:18) is told
in a vision to go out of Jerusalem "because they will not
receive your witnessing about Me". That the apostles
should be sent two and two is an indication that their
testimony was meant to be shown as agreeing or equal.
In Ac, it appears that Peter and John go about together, and the pairs that can be noticed in the naming
of the apostles (Simon and Jude) (Philip and Bartholo-
mew) may point to this custom also.

The second plane of witnessing is God's sphere. Jn
5:31–32 enunciates this theme. There is ANOTHER who
bears witness. From 5:36 it appears that the Father
bears this witness by giving into the hands of the Son
works (i.e. miracles) which He does on earth. In 5:37
there is added to this the witness that the Father gives
Himself through the words of God in the OT. As the
Jews who are being addressed have not this word "abid-

ing in them", they do not accept the Father's witness. Why is there the digression here about the witness of John the Baptist? Perhaps because in Jewish tradition (*Mishna*, Rosh-ha Shanah 1:7; 2:1–8) the witness of a father and a son to the new moon is said to need a third witness in corroboration. (The reproof to the Jews is in the indicative: "You search the Scriptures . . ." and not a command. It ends with what looks like a prophecy of Bar-Kokeba: "If another come in his own name, him you will receive.") The curious reading in 5:32, "You know", must be a change made in some of the MSS. such as *Sinaiticus* to point up still more the guilt of the Jews. Anti-Semitism is to be noticed in *codex Bezae* and is likely in the Armenian version and the African Old Latin.

Now the two witnessings by the Father amount to our old friends the arguments from miracles and prophecy, which go to establish the credibility of the claims of Christ. In Ac 10:43 and 14:3 we can see these in use at a much earlier stage of the preaching. In 14:3 (as in Mk 16:20) miracles are described as the witness of Christ to the preaching of the apostles, very much as John supposes them to be the Father's witness to the preaching of the Son.

In Jn 8:13–14 the argument is carried a stage further. Self-witness is admitted by Jesus, but this is said to be valid: "because I know where I came from and where I am going." These mysterious words seem to mean that Jesus is already on the plane of God's witnessing. Later He will say that God works the works that He himself does, and that He and the Father are one. Witness by a divine Person who is conjoined with a human nature is not the witness of a mere man to himself. That is the gist of the reply. The Jews receive this with mockery: "Where's your father?" (8:19, cf. 8:41),

which is very commonly taken as a jibe at the story of the Virgin Birth. (Hence in the *Talmud* the frequent confusion between Miriam, the mother of Jeshu, and Miriam the hair-dresser.[1])

In 7:18 and 28 hints are given to the Jews how they ought to prepare to receive rightly the witnessing of God. "In this shall you know that the Lord has sent me to do all His works", said Moses to Dathan and Abiron (Num 16:28), "that I do them not of myself." Echoing this, Our Lord says that he who speaks for himself is not true; his teaching should not be received. In a Rabbinical world this was clear, even though it might seem strange in days of scientific research where individual work is more highly esteemed. In Apoc 1:5 and 3:14 Jesus is given the title of "faithful witness", a title which echoes the Psalm (88:38 LXX). There are signs, e.g. in 1 Tim 6:13, that the role of Christ as witness was recognized long before John put pen to paper; it was part of the general NT idea that He shared in a common apostleship with the Twelve. They were "all in it together" and no Jewish charge of being a sole witness could be maintained. Behind Jesus and the apostles was the witness of the Father.

There was also (15:26–27) the witness of the Holy Spirit. That was to come at Pentecost, when the apostles would speak by the Spirit. The two verses are closely linked here: "Yes, and you it is who must and do bear witness." The present indicative is used, though the Vulgate has interpreted this with a future tense, and in form the Greek word used can also be taken as an

---

[1] Mary Magdalen almost certainly did not come from Magdala, for there is no evidence that there was such a place. On the other hand, the Greek word ἀπομαγδαλίς suggests that "the wiper" may have been a soubriquet given to Mary on account of her calling.

imperative. In the Synoptics (Mt 10:19–20 and parallels) the apostles had been promised that the Spirit would speak by them, but there had been no enlargement upon this promise. John has developed a canon of witnessing which he gives at length in 3 Jn 12, and it seems right to use that passage, as Hoskyns (p. 482) does, to throw light on this promise about Pentecost. "Demetrius has received the witnessing of all, and that of the very Truth: yea, and we ourselves bear him witness, and you know that our witness is true." The argument seems to be that John, speaking for the apostles, can lay claim to be speaking for the very Truth (see also p. 25). The saying of the angel to John in Apoc 19:10 that "you and your brethren have the witnessing to Jesus", and "the witnessing to Jesus is the Spirit of Prophecy" may be taken as a confirmation of the same idea. In the second century, before it became the custom to speak of New Testament and Old, the terms "prophets" and "apostles" were used to designate the two bodies of written evidence.

With all this emphasis on witnessing in the gospel, it does not seem unreasonable to take its concluding verses (21:24–25) as a final appeal to the same canon of evidence on the part of the author, as has already been noted in Chapter II. The Muratori fragment, in its account of the origin of the gospel of John, has dramatized this fact and makes up a whole incident in which Andrew is alleged to have proposed: "that John should write out everything on his own account while all of them looked over it" (*Ut recognoscentibus cunctis Ioannes suo nomine cuncta describeret*). The story is no doubt a fabrication, but it does show us what authority someone in the church at Rome in the late second century gave to John's gospel.

IV

John's Concept of Truth

TRUTH is the obvious counterpart of witnessing. Where perjury is absent, all witnessing is witnessing to the truth. Thus it is natural that John should speak (in 5:31–33) of truth as a characteristic of the witness of Christ, and again in the passages considered in the last chapter (8:13–17; 21:24). It is perhaps worth noticing that John the Baptist (5:35) and Christ (18:37) are said to have the same office, that of witnessing to the truth. This is reminiscent of the technique in Matthew, where an identical message ("The Kingdom of heaven is at hand") is recorded as coming from John, from Christ and from His apostles (Mt 3:2; 4:17; 10:7). That the original preaching of Christ had something of this burden within it may be seen from the one instance where the Synoptics use the word "true" (Mt 22:16, and the parallel Mk 12:14): "Master, we know that thou art true (truthful) and that thou teachest the way of God in truth." This opening of the Pharisee-Herodian gambit, which leads up to the question about the tribute-money, shows clearly that they thought this would be a good way of disarming suspicion; they must therefore have picked on a well-known characteristic of the preaching of Christ.

Not everything, however, is quite simple in this matter of witnessing to the truth. What are we to make of 3 Jn 12: "To Demetrius witness is borne by all, and by the Truth itself; yea ourselves bear him witness, and thou knowest that our witness is true." It has been said

by some that John, applying his rules for witnessing, could not have placed the witnesses in this order: first the people, then Christ, then himself as an Apostle, as that would be neither ascending nor descending order of merit. One may take leave to suppose that such nice- ties were not so freely observed in antiquity as they might be now. John could mean simply that Demetrius (who cannot be further identified, though some have said he is the Demas of Col 4:14 etc., and others want him to be the silversmith of Ac 19:24) was an original disciple of Christ and thus had the witness of the very Truth to himself. Some difficulty was felt in Syria about this verse, for the *codex Ephraemi rescriptus*, the text of Thomas of Harkel and other Syriac copies have added some words so as to read: "Witness is borne to him by all, and by the Church herself, and by the Truth and by John." Yet in view of the plain statement of Jn 14:16: "I am the Truth", it is reasonable to take this as an appeal to the witness of Christ as the very Truth.

Alongside the adjective denoting "true" (ἀληθής) in these passages John uses another (ἀληθινός) which means "genuine". The difference of meaning is rather fine (as both share certain areas of meaning) but it is of great importance. When one has to deal with Jewish minds brought up in what was to them the familiar study of typology, it must be obvious that Christians who argue with them need a word to denote the anti- type or realization of their types (see Justin, *dialogue* 41:4). The types can themselves be called true, in the sense that, e.g., Abraham sacrificing Isaac was not a mere ghost and was not content to go through a bit of miming, but, when one comes to the fulfilment of what he enacted in type, then that has to be called by a

31

stronger word, and for this John uses the word "gen-uine". Or at least he does so mostly. "I am the genuine Vine", says Christ in Jn 15:1. One can almost hear the overtones of reference to all that Israel had said about herself as the Vine. When the Jewish rebels in 67 began to strike coins for themselves, they put on them the legend: "Jerusalem the holy" and the outline of a vine with its branches. They would know what the "genuine Vine" meant on the lips of Christ. Jeremias had written of Israel: "I planted thee a vine all fruitful and genuine: how art thou turned to bitterness, thou estranged vine?" (2:21).

In Isai 49:6 the Servant is told: "Lo, I have set thee as a covenant to the People, as a light to the Gentiles, for thee to be unto salvation to the ends of the earth." John can therefore write in his Prologue: "Now there was the genuine Light, which enlightens every man, and it was coming into the world" (1:9). In his Epistle (1 Jn 2:8) he repeats this: "The darkness is on the way out, and the genuine Light is already shining." In Jn 6:32 the same word is used for the "genuine bread", where the type is set in contrast. "It was not Moses that gave you the bread from heaven, but My Father is offering you the genuine bread from heaven." Of course, Moses did bring down the manna from heaven, but that was only a type and not the reality; it was not final. A little later on (Jn 6:55) occur the words: "My flesh is meat indeed and my blood is drink indeed," and the adjectives here used are not the ones that mean "genuine" but "true". On this account some critics have sought to cut out the verse as spurious. One may think that this is somewhat hasty; John has to show that the language about meat and drink is true; it is to be taken literally. He has moved away from the contrast

of type and antitype which occupied him earlier; in fact there was not a ready type for the gift of the chalice to be found in the OT. (When the early Church looked for a "birthday of the chalice" she found it in the miracle of Cana and labelled Epiphany, when that event was commemorated, with the title "Birthday of the Chalice", as may be seen in the *Stowe Missal*). Hence John is keeping to his convention here by using the adjective for "true".

Sometimes the copyists have made things confused. Thus in Jn 8:16 the Bodmer papyrus reads: "My judgment is true"; *Vaticanus*, the *codex Bezae* and the Washington codex all have "genuine" for "true", and they have a following among the minor manuscripts, but it should be obvious that the papyrus has here preserved the correct reading. In 1 Jn 2:27 it is said that the anointing which Christians receive, "is true and is not a lie", but it has seemed good to Bultmann and others to suppose that here too John ought to have used the word for "genuine". Again one may ask what fulfilment of typology is to be expected here. The mention of "not a lie" should indicate what the contrast is. "Genuine" would be opposed to "preliminary", "typical", "non-final" and so on. Augustine on this passage (*tract.* 4:1 on the Epistles of John) says: "We who speak from without to your ears are like the gardener who applies his skill to the tree from without, but we cannot give it increase nor form its fruits. He who created you, redeemed you, called you and dwelleth in you by faith and by His spirit, if He speak not within you, it is in vain that we make a clamour outside. How is this to be seen? From the fact that though many listen to us, we do not persuade them all, but only those to whom God speaks within. Those who make room for God within

are those who have no room for the devil. The devil indeed desires to dwell in the hearts of men and to speak there words that will avail towards seduction, but what saith Our Lord Jesus? 'The prince of this world has been cast out.' Whence has he been cast out? Surely not from heaven and earth, nor outside the ramparts of this world but out of the hearts of those who believe."

Gradually this sense of "what is genuine, what is the fulfilment", comes in John to take on a connotation of "what is revealed", or "the full truth from God". Explicitly, in Jn 8:40, "the truth" is qualified with the words: "which I have heard from God." Truth in this sense must be revealed truth. Our Lord is not sparring with the Jews about His sincerity or His moral character here; it is His revelation, that fulfilment of what was promised to Abraham, that is at stake. One could almost have expected John to speak of "the genuine truth", but that would have required of him a more Hellenic cast of mind than he possessed.

The mention of truth in the sacerdotal prayer of Christ (Jn 17:17): "Sanctify them in the truth; thy word is truth", and 17:19: "that they also may be sanctified in the truth", seems to require this same sense of *"revealed* truth". From Jn 14:6 we know that Christ Himself is the truth, and thus the saying: "Thy word is truth" must be one of those Johannine sayings of double reference; the written word of God has been truth to Israel for the ages during which it has accumulated, but there is now a Living Word who is truth. As Irenaeus was to say: "In the name of Christ there are overtones; there is the one who anoints, Himself who is anointed, and the anointing that is the Spirit" (3:19:3). Revelation is not just an encounter with Christ, least of all an encounter in the Plotinian manner where no knowledge

passes and there is only a simple awareness of God, but it can be summed up in Christ, both the *theologia* or Trinitarian doctrine and the *dispensatio* or theology of the Incarnate Word.

There was in Hebrew a word *emeth* from the verb meaning to confirm or support (אָמֵן) and connected with *Amen* which was used to express an attribute of God (in the phrase Elohe-Amen: Isai 65:16). This phrase turns up again in Apoc 3:14, where it is a name for Christ. This stability or validity can come to mean something very like what we understand by the term "justification", but it is sometimes translated in the Greek OT by the word for truth. Hence Tobias 4:6 speaks of: "Those who do the truth making progress in their works"; in this sense Jn 3:21 can be taken. Paul (Eph 4:15) has almost the same idea. It is well known that the word for "faith" does not occur in John's gospel, though it comes four times in the Apocalypse and once (1 Jn 5:4) in the epistles. Perhaps he did not regard this technical term of the Christians as going back authentically to Christ. His term would be "doing the truth" or responding to the revelation of Christ. 1 Jn 1:6 recalls Nehem 9:33: "Thou art just in all that came upon us, for thou didst the truth and we committed sin." The idea of "walking in truth" (2 Jn 4 and 3 Jn 3) is a variant of this "doing", for to the Jewish mind conduct was a matter of walking (Halakha). What we should call conduct informed by the principle of faith was to them a manner of walking. Metaphors of staggering, of going astray, of slipping, are less familiar to our modern pedestrians than they were to users of the roads of Palestine.

V

John and the Gnostics

GNOSTICISM meant a private knowledge, not
accessible to the common man, that was concerned mainly with the two realities (vital for
any personal religion) of one's own soul and of God.
Paganism was in general a public religion that set far
more store by the exact performance of a liturgy than
by private prayer and communion with God. The Jews
on their part had something of the same tendency to be
content with public worship, and it is this which Our
Lord denounces in the Synoptic gospels when He re-
bukes the Pharisees for their formalism. It is therefore
possible *a priori* that both among Gentiles and among
Jews teachers and movements could arise in the first
century A.D. that would offer an escape from this
formalism by the imparting of a secret revelation, however it may have been derived. For the pagan there
were always the initiations into one or other of the
mystery cults, though these did not offer much of a
theology; one *did* things at the initiation and was then
assured of the proper guidance at the crisis of death and
passage to the other world, but this initiation did not
provide much food for thought or possibility of deeper
knowledge about oneself and God. It was still a liturgy,
but with active participation by the individual. The
Jews, having already the intricate worship of the
Temple and the rites of Passover and Tabernacles, did
not cultivate private, and still less secret, rites of worship. Even at Qumran, there cannot be shown any

clear proof of such rites; the dippings used there, in the tanks that are still preserved, were for purification, an extension of what went on at the Temple, and the blessings at meals were little more than what was normal.

A private revelation among the Jews, a *Bath-kol* for some special occasion,[1] was not thought to be uncommon, but the possession of a body of privately revealed truth was less frequently heard of. Hillel was said (TB *Sukkah* 28 a) to have had eighty disciples, thirty of whom were worthy that the Spirit of God should rest upon them (as it did upon Moses), thirty of whom were worthy that the sun should stand still for them (as it did for Josue), while twenty were ordinary.

Gradually there appear in Jewish tradition expressions such as "the work of the chariot" (Ezech 1:15–17) and "the work of creation" (Gen 1–2), which denote secret explanations of these most obscure passages of Scripture. It was even said (TB *Hagigah* 14 b) that these explanations should not be given in class, but to one disciple at a time. Here are the elements of Gnosis. But how soon did this appear in Palestine? Until recently one could not bring any firm evidence, save the isolated fact that Rabbi Johanan ben Zakkai (about the end of the first century A.D.) was said "to have known great matters", but now the Qumran documents provide further clues, while Jewish exegesis of the enclosed garden, the Paradise (פַּרְדֵּס) of Cant 4:13, was that it described secret knowledge and that four Rabbis had entered that garden: Akiba, Ben Zoma, Aher and Ben Azzai (all more or less from the end of the first century A.D.).

[1] A Bath-kol was a heavenly voice proclaiming God's will or His judgment, e.g. in Ezech 1:28.

37

The "Hymn of the Initiants" at the end of the *Manual of Discipline* has more than a little of Gnostic flavour (cf. pp. 128–9):

> Thou it is who hast taught all knowledge;
> and there is none to understand all Thy
> holy thought.

Further, the *Manual of Discipline* 3:20 (p. 53) has a passage praising the Fountain of Light which is promised to the faithful. The fragments of Scripture commentary which have survived at Qumran also indicate the kind of secret knowledge which would be imparted to the devotees there in the course of the long sessions of scripture-study which they undertook at nights (p. 49). "All who practise righteousness are under the domination of the Prince of Lights." This was an angel who is later called Metatron. He was credited in the Talmud (TB *Sanhedrin* 94 a) with a direct approach to God: "The Prince of the Universe said to God: 'Sovereign of the Universe: the earth hath fulfilled Thy desire for songs of praise'." When God wept for the destruction of the Temple, Metatron said: "Weep not Thou . . .". It was probably to this angel that Paul alluded in 2 Cor 11:14, where he said that Satan could transform himself, "as angel of light". Exod 23:21: "My Name is upon him", with the preceding verse: "Lo I send My angel before thy face", was taken by the Rabbis to refer to Metatron. That being so, and the use of this verse 20 (*via* Isai 40:3) in the beginning of the gospel (e.g. Mk 1:3) being taken into account, one may see how easy it would be for some Jewish-Christian of the latter part of the first century to think that all he had learnt about Metatron could be transferred to Our Lord, with the final result that he would then be forced

to admit that Jesus had not come in the flesh but was some angelic spirit. One can now see what John is about in 1 Jn 4:2 and 2 Jn 7, for no angel comes in the flesh.

Another danger John saw in this Jewish gnosticism was its tendency to lawlessness. "The truth shall make you free", is all very well, but it does not put its recipient above the ordinary laws of morality. That is why there is so much emphasis in 1 Jn on the keeping of the commandments as a sign of Christian profession (1 Jn 2:9; 1:6) and note in this second text the change of wording: "fellowship with *each other*" as a precondition of receiving His Blood.[1] "Keeping the commandments" is stressed in 1 Jn 2:3–5; 3:22–24; 5:3, just as it is in Jn 14:15; 14:21–24; 15:10; this word ($\tau\eta\varrho\varepsilon\tilde{\iota}\nu$) is not a Johannine coining, as it comes in Mt 19:17; 28:20. It is frequent also in Apoc 2:26; 3:3; 3:8–10; 12:17; 14:12).

Christ had said: "The sons are free" (Mt 17:24) in the episode of the temple-tax. This freedom was interpreted by Paul (Gal 3:4–14) as emancipation from the Law of Moses, while in Jn (8:32) Our Lord promises freedom to those who believe in Him and "abide in His word"; this will bring them to know the truth, and thus they will be free. They answer, even those who believe in Jesus, that they are children of Abraham and have never been slaves. The reply is the same that was made to John the Baptist by his hearers. Jesus explains that He is talking about freedom from sin. This idea of freedom coming out of knowledge does not reappear in the *Epistles* of John; perhaps this silence is significant.

There are three likely candidates for the work of

---

[1] *Codex Alexandrinus*, Tertullian, Clement, etc., have "with *Him*", and thus blunt the saying.

spreading some kind of Gnosticism among Jewish Christians: Simon Magus, Dositheus and Nicolas the deacon. Simon is met with in Samaria by Peter and John; hence John had early and first-hand knowledge of his ways. He is said by a wide and consistent tradition to have been the first heretic. He claimed to be all three Persons of the Trinity, the Son in Judaea, the Father in Samaria and the Spirit among the Gentiles (Irenaeus *adv. haer.* 1:16:1, H). He had a female companion, Helen, whom he called the first conception of his mind, claiming that she had come fully grown from his mind, like Athena from the head of Zeus. The angels were her children, who had conspired against her and imprisoned her till Simon came to the rescue. His followers were as free as children to do as they liked, since it was by his favour and not by good works that they would be saved. Magic was used to enliven his religion, and it may be that he encountered Peter in Rome.

Dositheus was a Samaritan. His disciples were known to Origen, even if he says with contempt that they do not number more than thirty in all. They had books and legends about him which said *inter alia* that he would not die (cf. Jn 21:23). Origen, commenting on Jn 4:25 says that Dositheus applied Dt 18:15 and Num 24:17 to himself as Messianic texts. These same texts were being discussed at Qumran, as we know from fragments found there. In the tradition Dositheus is a pre-Gnostic who has Menander and Saturninus as his disciples, but whether these are one after another in series, or contemporaries, no one can say for sure. Hence the *floruit* of Dositheus is somewhat uncertain, as between *c.* 60 and *c.* 90 A.D.

The Nicolaites are discovered at Pergamum by Apoc 2:14–16. They are compared to Balaam (Num 31:16),

who taught the Israelites to engage in idolatry and
fornication and to spare for future use the captive wives
of the Madianites, though Moses commanded them to
be slain. Pergamum was a place where involvement in
emperor-worship and pagan practices would be easy for
new Christians, and it may be that Nicolas the deacon
had gone there and persuaded them that this was the
way to increase their Gnosis. In the tradition there are
strange stories about his doings there but one cannot
entirely rely on these.

With these three near-Jewish sources of Gnosis
among the early Christians it does seem that there is as
much likelihood of the danger having sprung up first
among Jewish-Christian settlements. It is also to be
remarked that Simon and Dositheus have links with
Samaria, and so has Qumran, according to the opinion
of many today. Now the note of polemic against the
disciples of John the Baptist in the gospel of John may
be meant to guard against just this danger. They, like
the men of Qumran and these Samaritan teachers, may
have been inclined to go over to Gnostic ways later in
the first century, and John might then be said to be
seeking to correct a tendency which could not fail to be
dangerous.

Cyril of Alexandria, commenting on Jn 10:14 and
17:3, and Origen in a lengthy comment on Jn 8:19, are
careful to stress the fact that for the Jewish mind the
word "knowledge" had overtones which conveyed more
than the idea of intellectual comprehension; the OT
frequently appealed to an idea of knowledge by contact
(and particularly by sexual contact) which went beyond
the connotation of analysis into definitions. The Son's
knowledge of the Father is unique, but the reciprocity
that is implied in Jn 10:14 requires that some intimate

acquaintance with the Son and knowledge-by-partici-pation is in view for the Christian, and through the Son with the Father. The Gnostics were sure to abuse such language, but John had to use it, for it had been part of the original teaching of Jesus; at the same time as a precaution he hedged it round with demands for the keeping of Jesus's commandments.

VI

John and the Kerygma

I T is admitted by those who have looked carefully
into the parallels between John and the literature of
Qumran that the main resemblance is in the acceptance by both of the idea of a warfare of light and darkness. For both, God is the creator of the universe, and
thus there can be no fundamental dualism of good and
evil, but both conceive of the world as organized into
two camps under personal leadership. The difference
here is that, for John, Christ is the light of the world
(8:12; 12:36) and opposed to Him is the prince of this
world, whereas for the sectaries the two leaders are the
angels of light and of darkness, Metatron and A. N.
Other. For them the struggle is still evenly balanced,
though they have faith in a final victory; for John light
is already overcoming darkness and the eschatological
kingdom has begun (1 Jn 2:18). The contrast here is
well evidenced by the conversation with Martha
(Jn 11:24–27). That John is there not innovating upon
the traditional preaching of the apostles can be seen
by a glance at Ac 2:17, where Peter adapts a text from
Joel so as to emphasize that the last days have begun.
Both John and the men of Qumran hold that all men
are to be aggregated to one or other of the two camps,
but while at Qumran there is a wavering between free-
will and divine pre-destination, for John it is clear that
it is those who themselves refuse the light who will
remain in darkness. (Jn 3:19; 1 Jn 3:7–10). John
elaborates this in 1 Jn 3:2–3 by using the idea that the

43

act of seeing brings about an assimilation of the seer to the object of sight. We have seen Jesus (so as to believe in Him), and that has brought us a sonship of God (just as He is the Son of God), but God's great manifestation has not yet occurred. When it does, we shall be assimilated to God even more than we are now. Just as there was a preparation for "seeing Jesus", so (verse 3) there has to be for the greater manifestation. Qumran had nothing of all this. While for John (1 Jn 2:9–10) it is loving the brethren that marks out the sons of the light, at Qumran it is the doing of God's ordinances, and this means in practice obeying all the rules of the community. Anyone who enters and is unwilling to carry out the rules, "shall be cast out of that company as being one who has no share among the disciples of God" (*Zadokite work*, p. 81).

The source of much of this parallelism can be found in the OT. In Jer 7:18 the idolatry of Israel is described as worship of the army of the sky. Here is the one army for the warfare of light and darkness. In the speech of Stephen (Ac 7:42–43) this text is expanded by bringing to bear on it Amos 5:25–26. "You took up the tent of Moloch and the star of your god Raiphan, the images which you made for worshipping; and I will remove you to the other side of Babylon." Now this same text is glossed by the Qumran writers too, but in very different manner. Stephen had taken it from the LXX, but even then he changed Damascus to Babylon, presumably for reasons of his own. The *Zadokite work* says: "When Ephraim departed from Judah . . ., all who turned back were delivered to the sword, while those who stood fast were allowed to escape to the land of the North. It is to this that the text refers: 'I will exile Sikkuth your king and Kiyyun your image, the star of

your God, . . . beyond Damascus.' 'Sikkuth your king' refers to the books of the Law . . ., 'king' denotes the congregation, . . . 'Kiyyun your image' refers to the Books of the Prophets whose words the house of Israel has despised. As for the star, that refers to every such interpreter of the Law as indeed repairs to Damascus, as it is written: 'There shall rise up a star out of Jacob' . . .'' That Stephen and Qumran are both arguing about the meaning of a capital text shows that this text was vital in the days of the earliest apostolic preaching. Now John in Apoc has plenty to say about Babylon (14:8; 16:19; 17:5), all leading up to the great picture of the destruction of that city in Apoc 18, and always in connection with idolatry, as in Stephen's speech. John's preoccupation with the danger of idolatry is shown in 1 Jn 5:21. It is not mentioned explicitly in his gospel, but Jn 4:22–24 shows that the thought of it is not far away. It is obvious that the sectaries have twisted the text of Amos on account of its mention of Damascus, a place which was for some reason dear to them. Can it be that the Christian wording of this text (with Babylon for Damascus) in Stephen, and later in John, is due to a desire not to attack directly the people of Qumran by retaining the name of Damascus?

The "prophet like unto Moses" who was promised by Moses himself (Dt 18:15) is carefully and circumstantially identified with Christ by the gospel of Matthew, in accordance with the primitive preaching (Ac 3:22; 7:37) but after that the text is neglected. Mark and Luke have Our Lord designated by the crowds as being possibly "one of the prophets", but there is no mention of THE prophet, except perhaps at Lk 7:39, and this is textually very doubtful. Yet in Jn he comes into the limelight several times (1:21; 1:25;

1:46; 6:14; 7:40; 7:52) thus showing that John is keeping true to one of the main themes of the early preaching. That it should have seemed to lapse in the interim may be explained by the fact that for Paul there is a sharp antithesis between the Law and the Christian message, as can be seen at large in Romans, and this would naturally lead to a toning down of the importance of this particular line of apostolic preaching. John makes certain that we shall understand his return to the early tradition by the way he sets (in Apoc 15:3) Moses and Christ as parallel. The blessed sing "the canticle of Moses the servant of God and the canticle of the Lamb". The title of "servant of God" here given to Moses is one which, as we see from Acts, was in primitive use for Jesus. The only Scripture warrant for applying it to Moses is in Josue 14:7. But the Christian reader of the time would not miss the allusion. The verses which follow are not a citation of the canticle from Dt 32:4 etc., but a conflation of many words from the Psalms. John has not tried to compose the canticle of the Lamb, but he has perhaps indicated the lines on which early Christian hymns would develop. The Gentiles are mentioned indeed in the original Canticle of Moses, but only when it is said that God divided them up in order to set apart His chosen people.

From Jn 7:40 it follows that the multitude did not yet manage to identify the Prophet of Dt 18:15 with the Messias, but there was some speculation about this at Qumran, for a fragment found there has this text of Dt copied out as a sequel to Dt 5:25–6. It *may* have had as sequel the text about the star of Jacob (Num 24:17), though this is not proven. Anyhow, there was obviously much interest in the text at Qumran. The reading at Jn 7:53 which has been restored by the Bodmer papyrus

(P 66) has removed the difficulty (sometimes moved against the inerrancy of Scripture) about no prophet being said to come from Galilee when in fact Jonah certainly did so. The verse is a reply of the Sanhedrin to Nicodemus, who has just urged that they apply to Jesus the rules for evidence established in the OT. It is supposed to demolish at one go the claims of Jesus. Actually there is nothing in Dt 18:15–18 which rules out Galilee as place of origin for THE prophet, but one can easily see that "from amongst your brethren" could be taken to mean just that; Galileans were not pure Jews and so could not be counted as brethren.

Elsewhere in Jn (1:17; 3:14; 5:46; 7:23) there is a suggestion of parallelism between Moses and Jesus. The brazen serpent is a clear case. Jn 5:46 is a claim that Dt 18:15 does indeed apply to Jesus. In 7:23 the parallel is part of the complicated argument of that section, while in 1:17 the Law is contrasted with the grace and truth of Christ, as incomplete compared to complete.

VII

The Logos Doctrine

FOR John, the word *Logos* means the Person of
Christ, the Word of God. Now while it is true
that in this sense Logos is not used by the Synoptics, there are plenty of approaches to it in their work.
In Mk 4:14–20 the explanation of the parable of the
Sower has some interesting language. "The sower sows
the word . . . ; those by the wayside, where the word
is sown . . ., . . . Satan comes and snatches up the word
that is sown in them, . . . when there is persecution on
account of the word, they are scandalized." One cannot
stress normal phrases which are used here about
"hearing the word", but "persecution for the word" is
not normal, nor is "the sown word". The former of
these is found in Matthew but not the latter. Yet in a
catechetical passage of James (1:21) there is talk of
receiving the "engrafted word" (at baptism), and from
the parallel passage in 1 Pet 2:1 it looks as if the
"*rationabile lac*" there means "the milk that is the word".
There is plenty of evidence, then, that long before John
wrote the Christians were thoroughly familiar with
Logos as a term for "what they had received" or, as
we might say, their Christian faith. If now one takes
the Pauline position that he who is baptized puts on
Christ, or is incorporated into Christ, the logical conclusion from such a position is that the Word which we
receive, which is grafted into us, is Christ Himself. Why
not then say so?

In Mk 8:38 Our Lord has coupled His words and

Himself in an important saying: "Whosoever shall be ashamed of Me and of my words", and in this He is giving an obvious lead to the Church (which will have had to suffer much persecution before John comes to write) that such persecution may be for Him or for "the Word" indifferently. In John this idea of the words of Christ being closely associated with Himself is not lacking. Jn 6:63: "my sayings are spirit and life", matches 1:4: "In Him was Life." John has used another word ῥήματα and not Logos here, but in 12:48 he does not shirk the possibility of confusion. "He who cancels Me out and will not take My sayings has someone to judge him, the Word which I have spoken [and this time it is Logos] that will judge him at the last day." In Jn 15:7 the identification is complete. The theme is: "Abide in Me and I in you" (15:3). This is now taken to mean: "If you abide in Me and My sayings abide in you, ask what you will . . ." Jn 14:10 and 17:8 add to this that the sayings are those which Christ has received of the Father. In Dt 8:3: "the utterance of the mouth of God" (a text which is used by Christ in the temptation) the word (מוֹצָא) is for the Hebrew mind at once the rising of the sun, the rushing forth of water from a spring, the utterance of the mouth and the going forth in royal progress of the King. In fact, one is near to the verse of the carol: "The rising of the sun; the running of the deer, the coming forth of Jesus Christ and sweet singing in the choir." How deep in the Christian message this idea is may be seen from Lk 1:78, where the Knox version reads: "kindness of our God which has bidden Him come to us like a dawning from on high". This is too tame for what Zachary really said. "Mercy of our God, wherewith He shall rise and visit us from on high" (WV) is better.

49

The context of Dt 8:3 may have given John a start-ing-point for his meditations on the Logos. Here it is said that it is the utterance of God on Sinai that will save the people, and not the manna they have eaten in the desert. Christ's sayings have clearly this quality of salvation; they are the new Law, better than what was given to Moses on Sinai. Can it be that the primeval utterance of God, the word He spoke which made light (Gn 1:3), is now finding a parallel in what has hap-pened through Christ? That is what Jn 1 seems to suggest. The very first words "in the beginning" recall (and much more to a Jew, who knew of, and referred to, books by the opening word, in this case *Bereshith*, which means "in the beginning") the opening of Genesis, only now it is not the world at its beginning that is being scanned but the very life of God. Notice that John does not make Christ say: "I am the Logos", or put the technical term on His lips in the course of the gospel. Many critics speak and write as if he did and as if in doing so he had falsified the tradition of the sayings of Jesus.

What is given in the Prologue of John is his own meditation on the whole Christian message. There is a strophic form in the verses. That has been studied by Dr. Burney and Fr. Gächter. The clauses can be set in parallel, after the manner of a Jewish psalm. Did John make this arrangement, or is it a take-over from church-practice of the latter part of the first century? One cannot be certain that there is no borrowing, but given the extent of the correspondence between the Prologue and the gospel as a whole, it would require great bold-ness to charge John with borrowing here in his Pro-logue when he so clearly is not borrowing there.

When we look at 1 Jn 1:1, it must, I think, be

admitted that John has not borrowed his Prologue, but meditated it so as to make it what it is. It has been said by Hoskyns (p. 162) that John, "does not personify the Word of God. The Word had created him, not he the Word; and the Word of God had confronted the apostles in the Person of Jesus, the Son of God. The Word of God, petrified on Mt. Sinai, was incarnate in Jesus Christ." (The antithesis of stone and flesh is familiar from Jeremias and elsewhere in the OT and surely it is this antithesis that is being suggested by the emphasis on flesh in 1 Jn.) The evangelist saw in his meditations that this, with its negative and positive implications, was the very heart of the faith of the apostles.

In the course of his gospel he draws out what is involved in Jesus as the Word of God. He is the Light, the Life, the Truth, the Bread of Heaven, the Way, the Door, the Good Shepherd and the Resurrection. These are in the 4th gospel no ragged independent fragments, whirling about in their own right and of their own initiative. The figure of Jesus as the embodiment of the glory of the Word of God controls the whole matter of the Christian religion. (Hoskyns, *ibid.*)

The OT had come near to personifying Wisdom. The passages in Prov 8:12–36 and 9:1–6 are proof of this. The claim to have been there before the world was, to have been with God putting order into everything, all this would raise in a Jewish-Christian mind the question: "Can we say that Jesus in His divine life was thus pre-existing, if this is said in the OT of Wisdom?" The other passage, about Wisdom building her house and inviting to the banquet, has sufficient resemblance to the parables which Christ spoke about Himself in the Synoptic gospels to make the parallel the more obvious.

The further question (which was raised when Arius began to use this text to claim that the Son was a creature) namely: "Is the Son Begotten or Made?", was also envisaged by the Prologue, and in saying: "The Word was with God," John answers his own question. Not but what the Arians were to try to get their view of the matter out of Jn 1:3–4, but that must be treated later.

John had surely had some revelation which guided him in his meditations, for in Apoc 19:13 he speaks of his vision of the rider of the white horse, how He had diadems on his head and a name that none knew save Himself and then he adds: "and His Name is Logos of God." The vision may have owed something to Wisdom 18:15, where one may read: "Thy all-powerful Logos from heaven out of the royal throne drove down to earth, a sharp foeman bearing as a keen sword Thy unescapable command, and there He filled everything with death . . ."

VIII

The Concept of Life

THE average Jewish idea (in the first century A.D.) of the origin of human life from God was expressed by what was told about the mother of the Maccabees (2 Macc 7:22) as she spoke to her sons before their martyrdom: "It was not I that gave you spirit and life, nor did I set in orderly growth the elementary structure of each of you. The creator of the universe, who fashioneth the origin of man and hath found out ways of birth for all things, Himself in His mercy offers you now a return of your spirit and life seeing that you value His law above your own life." When Gamaliel II was questioned by the Sadducees about the power of God to raise the dead, he replied by quoting Dt 31:16 (i.e. a passage where God tells Moses he is to die, but which is to be taken along with Dt 32:39 "I slay, and I make to be alive") and Isai 26:19 "The dead shall rise up and those in the tombs shall be roused and those that live on the earth shall rejoice. The dew that is from Thee is healing unto them . . ." [1]

The Talmud also reports a supposed dialogue of this Gamaliel's daughter with Hadrian, in which she shows him by an argument *a minore ad maius* that God who gives the life of the human body at conception can also give back life to the dead. John shows Christ claiming this power as His right (Jn 5:21–25) but with a subtle overtone of meaning. The life that He can give is not

[1] Fr. Sutcliffe in his book *The OT and the Future Life* takes this to refer to a return from captivity.

only the raising to life of the dead body, but also a quickening of the soul to a new life, which later generations of theologians would call supernatural. Both senses are mixed in this passage: "The Father raises the dead and gives life, and the Son too gives life to whom He would." This verse is on the ordinary level of Jewish understanding. The audience would see in it a claim of Jesus to have the power of the Father, but they would take this claim to refer to the giving of physical life to the dead. None the less, the Syriac version (in the Curetonian MS.) has put: "the Son giveth life to those who believe in Him"; thus anticipating what is to be said in verse 24 "He that heareth My word, and believeth in Him that sent Me, hath eternal life and cometh not to judgment but hath passed over from death to life." The indication that this claim is true is given in verse 25 by an appeal to the fact that soon, and even now, there will be some that will be raised from the dead by the Son of God. This clearly looks ahead to the raising of Lazarus, while also looking back to Dan 12:2, which is the one OT place generally accepted as teaching a future life.

For the Synoptic tradition there was the conversation with the Pharisees about God being the God of the living and not of the dead, and then the brief mention of the phenomena (Mt 27:53) that occurred at the Resurrection, when some of the dead went before Him into the Holy City. For the Synoptics there was also the raising of the daughter of Jairus and that of the widow's son at Naim. But these are not connected with the preaching of a new doctrine of eternal life. The very word "eternal" that describes it is allowed a mention there only in the question of the young man about the way to obtain it (Lk 18:18 and 30). Luke has adapted

the story of the lawyer who asked about the great commandment in this sense too (Lk 10:25 and 28).[1] There is therefore just enough in the Synoptic tradition to let us know that John is not falsifying the primitive Christian message with his teaching on eternal life. In spite of the backwardness of the OT in conveying the message of the resurrection of the body, it is clear (from the Talmud and from Paul) that in the first century A.D. there were plenty of Jews who accepted this teaching avidly, even though the official line of the Sadducees was to reject it; but John is going beyond that kind of eternity to a new sense of eternal life. God the Father has eternal life in Himself and He has given this to the Son (5:26).

In this basic revelation of the inner life of the Trinity John can see something that it is given to man to share. "That which came-to-be-in Him was LIFE" (1:3-4). After the Prologue has spoken of the life of the Trinity, of how the Word was with God, there comes the tremendous mystery of our "coming-to-be-in Him." The text of Jn 1:3-4 is on the face of it open to two different ways of interpretation, and that by a defect or default of punctuation. By the time of Chrysostom it had become usual to punctuate as the Vulgate now reads, but this was a change expressly made to avoid an heretical meaning. Those who denied that the Holy Spirit was God said that this verse proved it; "What has come to be was the life in Him", i.e. the Spirit, or Life dwelling in the Son, was a creature, a something that had come to be. The Church altered the manner of reading the words in order to check the heresy. But, of

[1] One may note that Luke has added, quite in keeping with the context, the story of the Good Samaritan after this questioning episode; this may be a piece of his Johannine material.

all the thirty-eight places where the text is known to have been used before the Council of Nicaea, there is none that had that way of phrasing it. "What has come-to-be-in Him" (neuter) is a general phrase, due for further elaboration later; it covers all those who hear Christ's word and believe in Him, as explained in 5:24 . . . etc. Here again the meaning is on two levels. Creation is a giving of life, and that can be attributed to the Son (cf. Col 1:16 and Prov 8:30 with Wisd 7:12) so that one might truthfully say that all that came to be was living through the Son, but the more particular sense is that all those of whom it can be said that they are in Him (or have come-to-be-in Him) have supernatural life.[1] Origen put this bluntly: "If we understand the life that comes to be in the Logos, if we know Him who said: 'I am the Life', we shall assert that no one of those outside the faith of Christ is alive, but all who live not to God are corpses."

The fullest definition of what John understands by eternal life is given in 17:2–3: "Thou gavest Him power over all flesh, that all which Thou hast given Him, to them He will give eternal life; and this is eternal life, that they may know Thee the one genuine God and Him whom Thou hast sent, Jesus Christ." John never uses the double title for Christ, save here and 1:17. (It is found in his Epistles several times and in the title of the Apoc thrice.) The contrasting phrases: "all flesh" and: "what Thou hast given Him", give emphasis to the gap between the abundance of God's grace and the poverty of man's response. "God did not make death and does not rejoice in the ruin of the living. The life

[1] This view of Jn 1:3, advocated by the present writer in *Clergy Review* 38 (1953), 539–48, is now adopted by B. Vawter in *Catholic Biblical Quarterly* 25 (1963), 401–06.

is the light of men, for just as the Son is the Light of the Father, so He is the Life of the Father to whom that Father hath given life; and all those that have been given to Him, to them He gives eternal life." Thus an ancient Latin commentary on the Creed written *c*. 375–400.

In Apoc 1:9–10 John says that he had "come-to-be-in spirit on the Lord's day", after having "come-to-be-in the island of Patmos." This double use of the phrase indicates the sense in which John would use it habitually. Further, in Rom 16:7 we are told by Paul that Andronicus and Junias are distinguished among the apostles and that they have "come-to-be-in Christ" before Paul himself. The likelihood that Andrew and John are here referred to under more elaborate Greek names is great,[1] not only on the hypothesis that the salutations here given are meant for Ephesus and not for Rome, but also by the fact that double names (Eleazar and Lazarus, Silas and Silvanus etc.) were common for Jews who moved about in the Dispersion. The local sense of coming-to-be-at Rome is used by Paul in 2 Tim 1:17; otherwise he does not use "come-to-be-in"; he has one or two uses of "happen in the case of", e.g. 1 Cor 9:15, but it looks as if he picked up from another the phrase "come-to-be-in Christ". Had he heard John say this of himself? The phrase is a Semitism in Greek and may be found in the OT from Exod 4:4 and 13:9 onwards.

The "water of Life" was an idea familiar in the East, where it is found as early as the Babylonian mythology. In the OT (Osee 14:6, and cf. Isai 26:19) "the dew of God" is spoken of as the power that vivifies. Now in

[1] This was first suggested by Fr. John Donovan, S.J., in his *Authorship of the Fourth Gospel* (1935).

57

Apoc 11:6 it is said of the Two Witnesses that they have authority to close the heavens so that the rain shall not bedew the earth in the time of their prophesying. This may be a symbolic statement about the right of the Church to control access to the means of eternal life. The Witnesses are in some aspects a reminiscence of Peter and Paul, though they look forward to the whole race of persecuted heralds of the gospel.

The term "genuine life", though not found in John's writings does come into use very soon. In the Epistle of Ignatius to the Ephesians (7:2) there is a credal passage where Jesus is described as God in man's nature, "in death genuine life". In the same Epistle (11:1) it is said to be enough for any Christian "to be found in Christ Jesus unto the genuine life." This is practically an exhortation to them "to come-to-be-in Christ" and so to have life. It is the characteristic of Ignatius that, though he does not quote John verbatim, he shows his familiarity with many a Johannine saying, in the same manner as here. It has also been suggested by Peterson and others that "those who live" in 1 Thess 4:15 is a synonym for "Christians". In Acts Christianity is referred to as "this way", and the term to a Jewish mind was equivalent to a manner of life.

In the Synoptics there are several anticipations of the Johannine teaching about life. "Entering into life" is the Synoptic term (cf. Mt 7:14; 18:8–9; 19:16–20; 25:46 and parallels). The greater precision which the teaching of John introduces (3:36 and 5:24 especially and 1 Jn 3:14) is to make it clear that eternal life is already begun for the Christian; grace is the incipient form of glory, as theologians would say later on. In the Synoptics this is left vague and undefined, though not contradicted. How different this is from the current Greek and Jewish

philosophizing may be seen from the passage of Philo (*Quis rerum divinarum heres*, 45) where a triple notion of life is expounded. For Philo there is the physical life of begetting, that ends with death, there is a God-ward life, and there is another form which is on the boundary between these two. This intermediary is quite unlike John's notion of eternal life begun here below; Philo would not have dared to propose that, but the everyday Christian, who had been given milk and honey after his baptism to signify to him that he had now entered into a Promised Land, knew what was meant by the beginning of eternal life. One may see it writ large in the *Odes of Solomon*, which are baptismal hymns roughly contemporary with the writing down of John's gospel.

IX

The Light of the World

"STREAKS of lightning will flash from one end of the world to the other, growing ever brighter until the era of darkness is brought utterly to an end . . . God's exalted grandeur will give light for evermore, shedding on all the sons of light peace and blessing." So the Qumran Scroll entitled *The war of the sons of light and the sons of darkness* (p. 261). Isai 60:19-20 had already outlined what was to come: "No more shalt thou have the sun as a light by day; nor shall the moon's rising lighten thee in the night; but Jahwe shall be for thee an eternal light and thy God thy adornment. For thy sun shall not set nor thy moon suffer eclipse, and the days of thy mourning shall have been completed." When one recalls that this chapter of Isaias (in the LXX) begins with the redoubled exhortation: *Photizou, photizou, Jerusalem,* where the verb means, "be enlightened", that for the early Christians it provided the term for "to get oneself baptized", the possibilities of this light-imagery being taken over extensively by Christian writers are obvious. One can see the term *photismos* used for baptism as early as Hebr 6:4 and 10:32 [cf. also 2 Cor 4:6 and 2 Tim 1:10].

The Shekinah is a term never used in the OT but made up by Rabbinic commentators to mean, "the majestic presence or manifestation of God which has descended to dwell among men" (*shâkan* = to dwell). This presence is quite naturally held to be disclosed by

light, by a great light. The burning bush, the pillar of cloud that was of fire by night, or the light over the Ark when Israel took it out to war (1 Kg 4:4), all these were occasions when the Shekinah was amongst them. Now in Jn 1:14 there seems to be an attempt to make of this Jewish concept a vehicle for transmitting the Christian theology of the Incarnation. "The Word was made flesh"; that statement gives rise to the very term *Incarnation*, while its complement: "And dwelt amongst us", could have given rise to a parallel term *Shekination* but did not. John has picked on a Greek word (σκηνόω), which means "to pitch one's tent", to set up a Tabernacle or an abiding-place for the glory of God. John had previously viewed the mystery in Apoc 21:3: "Behold the Tabernacle of God with men, and He shall make His dwelling with them". Joel 4:17 [LXX] foreshadowed this: "Know ye that I your God will make my dwelling in Sion the holy mountain . . ." (= 3:17 in Vulg). In Apoc 7:15 is a foreglimpse of the same mystery, while he can write in 21:23 "The city needeth not sun nor moon to shine in it, for the glory of God hath illuminated it and the Lamb is the lamp thereof." One must notice here the linking in John's sentence of *Shekinah* and *photismos*, or, in other terms, Incarnation and baptism.

If, then, there is a peculiar link between baptism and the presence of God with His people in the Christian Church according to John, why does he say (1:9) that the true Light illuminates every man who is born into the world? A contemporary of John, whom we have cited already, Rabbi Gamaliel the Younger, had said: "The sun illuminates the whole world, but how much rather the Shekinah." (TB *Sanhedrin* 39 a). If one pursues through the gospel the passages where John

introduces Christ speaking of Himself as Light of the world, it is possible to see the elements of an answer. There are two levels, or two incidences, of this Light. "I am the Light of the world; he that followeth Me walketh not in darkness, but *shall have* the Light of life." "Following" comes first, then "having the Light" (in fuller measure) comes after. In 9:5 there is another limitation: "What time I am in the world, I am the Light of the world. There cometh night when no man can work." This really looks back to 1:9 in its proper Greek construction, where the sense required is: "There was the true Light, which illuminates all men, and it was making its way into the world." Yet although this diminishes in some measure the generality of the saying, it does not quite extinguish it. And in any case the dogmatic tradition which has been built up in the West by generations of theologians following the Vulgate rendering, shows that there must be a true sense in which the Light that is Christ is for all men. One can say in vague terms that all men have grace offered to them, somehow or other, and that all grace in this dispensation is the grace of Christ. John's final passage (12:46) adds a little to this picture: "I, Light, have come into the world that everyone who believeth in Me should not remain in darkness; and if any man hear My word and keep it, I do not judge him." (Note that the negative is omitted from before the word "keep" in the Bodmer papyrus P 66 and in D, along with many minuscules; the idea that the true Christian does not need judging is implied in 1 Jn 4:17 and is said openly at Jn 5:24). John simply bears witness to the mystery of the universal offering of Light and the partial diffusion of it, in the passage 12:36–46, where he speaks on his own. After Jesus' appeal: "While you have the Light, believe in the Light

that you may become Sons of the Light", there follow
the personal reflections of John:

> The miracles of Christ were largely in vain, for, after all,
> that was what one ought to have expected from what hap-
> pened to the prophets. Isaias saw the Shekinah (Isai
> 6:1–6), and yet he also saw this fearsome mystery. Still
> some *did* believe, though they seem to have remained half-
> way in their belief, and in the end this was their own
> fault. They loved a counterfeit Shekinah that was human
> and not the divine Shekinah.

It may be asked why, if John sets so much store by his
teaching on the Shekinah, there was no great body of
doctrine built up on it in the patristic age and handed
down to us. One answer could be, in three words, the
Gnostic danger. "The gospel-light descended upon
Jesus, son of Mary, through whom it is being mediated
to the spiritual part of the world," said Basilides. All
manner of ways of destroying the reality of the flesh of
Christ could be opened up by sayings like that. Chrysostom might urge later on that nothing dwells in itself,
thus suggesting that one should regard the Shekinah
as the divinity of Christ and its tabernacle should be
considered to represent His humanity, but, once the
Jewish mentality was gone from the Church, there was
little prospect of that line of thought bringing much
relief.

Justin Martyr became a Christian at Ephesus some
thirty years after John's death. It is then worth noting
that in his *Apology* he gives us some remarkable insights
into what the early Christians were discussing. One of
these is the interpretation of some strange OT texts such
as the Oracle of Jacob about the future hero who should
tether his colt to the vine-branch and dip his garment

in the blood of the grape (Gen 49:11). This is what Justin says:

> What the Spirit of God has called "*garment*" in the words of the prophet means the men who believe in Him and who have within them the divine seed which is the Logos. The expression "blood of the grape" means that the one who is to appear will have blood, and that not from human seed but from the divine power. (*Apol* 32:9.)

Later he says: "The power of God coming upon the virgin overshadowed her and made her to bear a child while being a virgin." This power he interprets to be the Logos (*Apol* 33:4 and 6). Wine was for Hippolytus the accepted symbol of the divinity; wine and garment therefore suggested to the second-century Christian mind the two natures of Christ. This pair of images may have come to supplant the Shekinah-and-tabernacle pair which were thought to be capable of misleading men in a Gnostic-ridden age. It is to be noted that the gospels themselves in their account of Palm Sunday make no attempt to bring in this passage from Gen 49 about tethering the colt.

X

The Sign of the Temple

IN Mal 3:1 (according to the LXX) one reads: "And straightway there will come to His own temple the Lord whom you seek and the Angel of the Covenant whom you desire. Lo, He cometh, saith the Lord almighty. And who shall withstand the day of His entrance?" It would seem to be this verse which caused John to transpose the event of the cleansing of the temple from the place where it is recorded by the Synoptics (either Palm Sunday, as Mt, or the day following, as Mk) and to put it at the beginning of the public life. Thus the significance of the "straightway" in Malachy was brought out. As Fr. Martindale says: "It seems unlikely that our Lord would have inaugurated His ministry by so drastic an action with nothing leading up to it. In Galilee He entered almost imperceptibly upon His ministry, unlike the sensational Baptist." One detail in Mk (11:16) shows the eyewitness; it is just such a detail that a young boy would recall: "He made to forbid anyone to carry a pitcher through the Temple." No short-cuts; that would be hard on people who were accustomed to them. Mark, who is certainly on the spot at the time of the Passion,[1] might not have been there to observe this detail one or two (or three) years before. Again, if there had been two cleansings of the temple, it seems incredible that

[1] This assumes that the young man of Mk 14:51–52 is Mark himself. Converging probabilities point to this conclusion, especially the stylistic similarity of Ac 12:12–17 and Mark's gospel.

this should have been passed over in the Jewish accusations at the time of the trial. Hoskyns adds another reason: "The fourth evangelist is concerned more with the meaning of the words and actions of Jesus than with their original setting or relative order. Understood as he understood it, the cleansing of the Temple provided the key to a proper understanding both of the quite fundamental controversy of Jesus with the Jews and of the implications of discipleship." (p. 198.)

It should be noticed that the words of our Lord about destroying the temple, which John alone records as spoken at the cleansing, are quite clearly presupposed by what the Synoptics say of the accusations made at the trial (Mt 26:61; Mk 14:58) and by the mocking at the Crucifixion (Mt 27:39; Mk 15:29). It may be that the Synoptics did not want to suggest, by reporting the actual utterance of the words, that there was even a semblance of justification in the charge that was brought.

It is curious and worth noticing that there is independent Jewish evidence that something of the kind was said by someone just about forty years before the destruction of the temple. The Talmud reports that Rabbi Zadok began at that time a fast intended to avert the destruction of the temple. What drove him to it is not clearly put, though one can very well explain his action by supposing that he was impressed by what Jesus had said and done on this occasion.

J. Jeremias sees in the episode a stylized parallel with the Cana miracle, which precedes it in Jn 2; there the new wine, here the temple purified. Both episodes would be meant to show how the faith of the disciples in Jesus was strengthened, for that is the conclusion to which John comes at the end of each narrative (2:12; 2:22). The verse of Ps 68:10 which John says the dis-

ciples called to mind (presumably after it was all over) and which confirmed their faith, is by tradition the one which gives the keynote to the whole Passion liturgy, being the antiphon of the first psalm of *Tenebrae* of Wednesday in Holy Week. Within John's narrative there is another scriptural allusion, not quite full enough to be an explicit quotation, referring to Zach 14:21. "There shall not be a Canaanite (i.e. a merchant) any more in the house of the Lord almighty on that day." This is the last verse of the prophecy of Zachary and in the Hebrew Bible it is followed by the prophecy of Malachy. John may have seen the connection here.

We have reason enough to think that a new liturgy was a-coming with the coming of Christ, though immediately after the Resurrection it was not accepted by the apostles that this had to be. Stephen indeed shows more complacency (Ac 7:44–46) in the tent of the wilderness than in the temple and has changed (7:7) the wording of Exod 3:12 from "this mountain" to "this place". John had seen in the visions of the Apocalypse that there was an altar in heaven (Apoc 6:9; 8:3; 9:13; 14:18 and 16:7), whether the golden altar of incense or the altar of holocausts, and there was a temple, but that temple was the Lord Himself (21:22). Did not this follow, in a manner, from what He had spoken about destroying the temple of His body? John may be thought not to have so clear a concept of Christ as the altar as that implied in Hebr 13:10 or Hebr 9:1–4 for instance; the heavenly liturgy that is glimpsed in Apoc 7:9–12 or 22:1 is all in terms of "the throne of God and the Lamb". But from 8:3 it follows that there is a golden altar before the throne, and in 6:9 this is somehow associated with the prayers of saints and martyrs.

In early tradition there is plenty of evidence of the

idea of an heavenly altar: Irenaeus (*adv. haer.* 4:31:5) said: "There is an altar in heaven; for thither our prayers and petitions are directed." There is a temple too, for John said that he saw it opened and that it came down from heaven: Apoc 11:19 and 21:3. It must be noted that in paragraph 3 of his passage Irenaeus speaks of the offertory, in paragraph 4 of the consecration, and now in paragraph 5 of there being a heavenly altar. This suggests that already the Canon of the liturgy had some prayer like our *Supplices* or at least something expressing the same motif. Victorinus of Pettau thought that the Holy Spirit took up our prayers just as the high priests had taken, once a year, the blood of the sacrifice to within the veil. Hermas says: "The prayer of a wicked man has no power to go up to the altar of God." Gradually this idea is overlaid by the action of a false tradition started through a misunderstanding of a passage in Ambrose.[1] In Syriac use, however, the idea that the sanctuary of a church is heaven, the steps down to the communion-rails, paradise, the walk from there to the central throne, the "way to heaven", and the throne itself, Jerusalem, which is in the centre of the nave (which stands for the flat earth); all this perpetuated the idea of a heavenly altar for Eastern Christians.

The Jewish belief (2 Macc 2:5) that the Ark and golden altar had been hidden at the time of the Captivity, not to be revealed till the end of the world, would have been part of the mental outlook of the apostles and the early Jewish Christians.[2] Hippolytus says: "The Ark

---

[1] See the discussions. v. "Altar" in *Catholic Dictionary of Theology*, I.

[2] The Moslems took the story from the Jews and profess to believe, on the authority of a cousin of Mahomet, that the Ark is at the bottom of the lake of Tiberias and will not come up until the end of the world.

from incorruptible wood was the Saviour Himself. That incorruptible and undecaying tabernacle of His declares itself by this that it produced no corruption of sin. The sinner makes confession saying: 'My sores are putrified and corrupted because of my foolishness'; but the Lord was without sin, being in His human nature from incorruptible wood, i.e. from the Virgin, and being sheathed as it were with the pure gold of the Word within and of the Spirit without." Hippolytus went further than Irenaeus who had said: "As the Ark was gilded with fine gold within and without, so the body of Christ is pure and bright, adorned within by the Word and without by the Spirit . . ." Gregory Thaumaturgus said of Our Lady in his sermon: "She is an honourable temple of God and a shrine most pure and a golden altar. . . . She is the incense of oblation and a precious vase bearing the true nard, yes and the priestly diadem. . . ." Then Athanasius, in his newly found sermon which has been published from a Coptic text in *Le Muséon* 71 (1958) 216: "To what shall I liken thee among all creatures? O ark of the new covenant, clad on all sides with purity in place of gold, the one in whom is found the golden vase with its true manna, i.e. the flesh in which lies the godhead. . . . If I say that heaven is high, *it is not thy equal*, for it is written (Isai 66:1): 'Heaven is My throne', while thou art the resting-place of God."

So early a testimony of the doctrine of the bodily Assumption deserves to be noticed more than it has been hitherto.[1] It falls into line with the earlier witness of Hippolytus, just cited, about the Ark made from

[1] If Athanasius had believed that the body of the Blessed Virgin was in an earthly tomb, he could hardly have said (in the present tense) that she *is* the resting-place of God.

incorruptible wood, and it also fits the early liturgical use of Ps 131:8 as a text that praises the Blessed Virgin. The Armenian lectionary has this verse as the Introit for the feast of our Lady on August 15: "Arise, Lord, into Thy rest, Thou and the Ark of Thy sanctification." There are signs that this lectionary goes back to the fourth century in its choice of passages, and it would not be surprising if this understanding of the Ark in heaven as a figure of the Virgin had some connection in the early tradition with the explanation of what John saw in Apoc 11:19, when the temple was opened in heaven and the Ark was seen therein.

XI

The Keeper of the Gate

I N that Christian romance called the *Clementine Recognitions* Peter is represented as praying for the help, "of Him who alone is not shut out of the house that is full of smoke, that He may come nigh and open the door of the house in order that the smoke that is within may be extruded, while the light of the sun that is without may shine within." The parallel document called the *Homilies of Clement* (1:18; GCS 42:32) has the same episode, but more expansively; the house full of smoke is the world, the smoke being covetousness, lust, brazen shamelessness and so on, and it is there said that someone inside must open the house to let the smoke escape. This can be done by the true prophet and none other; he alone is able to enlighten the souls of men. Thus from the end of the second century we have an illustration of the use made of the door-keeping image among the Jewish Christians who cherished these writings. Hegesippus is cited by Eusebius (HE 2:23) as telling how James, bishop of Jerusalem, was repeatedly asked by the Jews: "Who is the door of Jesus?" One answer of James is given to the effect that Jesus is the Saviour, but, when the question is put just before his martyrdom, James says: "Why do you ask me about Jesus the Son of Man? Why, He is sitting in the heavens on the right hand of the great Power, and He is going to come on the clouds of heaven." From all this it would seem that the image of

Jesus as the door was current before 60 A.D. and was elaborated in the Jewish-Christian catechesis.

In John's elaborate parable of the Shepherd and the Door of the Sheep (a twofold role which Our Lord claims for Himself) appeal is being made to what must have been familiar to a Jewish audience. Both claims are made twice (Jn 10:7 and 9 for the Door of the Sheep, and 10:11 and 14 for the Good Shepherd). In Nehem 3:1 to 31 (= 2 Esdr 13:1 to 31, in the LXX) there is the story of the rebuilding of the gates of the holy city: "Then Eliasib the high priest arose and his brethren the priests and they built the flock-gate. They sanctified it and set up the doors thereof." The account goes on to enumerate the other gates: the fish-gate; the watergate to the eastward, the dunghill-gate, the gate of the valley, the gate of the fountain, the horse-gate and the judgment-gate. The account ends with the words: "Within the chamber of the corner of the flock-gate the goldsmiths and the merchants built." It is obvious from this that the work began and ended with the flock-gate. Was Jesus therefore asserting by his comparison that He was the cornerstone of the new Jerusalem? That John had seen the gates of the new city in Apoc 21:13 makes this probable. In Jn 5:1 the pool at Bethsaitha is mentioned as being near the sheep-gate. This pool has been found in recent times: "two all-but-square pools cut deep in the rock and girdled by porticoes of Hellenistic type with a fifth portico forming a gangway between the pools, the water for the pools being brought in stone pipes from the temple-area or beyond." Before it became a Roman-style lido, the pool may have been meant for washing the animals, sheep and oxen, that came into the temple for sacrifice. If, then, the sheep-gate is part of the parable, it is not quite so strange

that Our Lord should go on immediately to the talk about laying down His life.

According to 10:6 the disciples had not understood the opening of the parable about the Shepherd. Hence the new start with a slight variation in 10:7 where the figure of the Door is introduced, which limits for a moment the role of Jesus to a passive one of giving protection (safety from the wolf or robber). When that is understood, the more active role of leading out to pasture can be contemplated; it is hinted at in 10:9 (though a door cannot of itself give pasture) but it comes out more fully in 10:14, which takes up again what is said in 10:4. Yet, even so, it is the protective role which comes uppermost (10:13 and 15) through the contrast with the hireling. One must add that in the parallel passage of 21:15–19, where Peter is set up as Shepherd, it is this protective note which comes uppermost again: "as the Father sent His Son to be the good Shepherd of the sheep and to lay down His life on their behalf, so the Son sends His disciple to be both Shepherd and Martyr, signifying by what manner of death he was to glorify God" (Hoskyns, p. 556). This was commented on by Augustine (*tract.* 47 on John). After quoting 1 Jn 3:16, he says: "If you sit at the table of a mighty man, understand well what is put before you, and put in your hand, knowing that such things you too must provide [citing the LXX of Prov 23:1]. You know what the table of the mighty man is. There is placed the Body and Blood of Christ. He who goes thither must himself provide such things. What does this mean? Just as He laid down His life for us, so too should we, to profess our faith and to build up the city of God, lay down our lives for the brethren. Thus to Peter, when He wished to make him the good shepherd—though not for Peter's self but for

the whole body of the Church—He said: 'Peter, lovest thou me? Feed my sheep . . .' and when He had three times commended to him the feeding of His sheep, He said: 'When you were younger you put on your girdle yourself and went where you pleased, but when you are grown old . . .' Feeding the sheep involves laying down one's life."

But who are the hirelings who come up so frequently in the passage? "All who came before Me are thieves and robbers", says 10:8.[1] The text has been tampered with, as it suited Marcion too well, for he could use it to throw overboard the whole OT. Some omitted the word "all" and there is a trace of this remedy in Didymus of Alexandria and *codex Bezae*, while the omission of "before Me" can be traced through a great many MSS. The Bodmer papyrus (P 66) has the full text and it is this that must be interpreted. John Chrysostom took it to mean that the rebels listed in Ac 5 (Judas of Galilee and the like) were the thieves, and to them the sheep did not listen. He would exclude the Prophets from the scope of this verse. So would Augustine (*tract.* 45); he says: "Are the Prophets thieves and robbers? *Absit.* They did not come before Him, but they came with Him. He who was to come sent His heralds in advance, but the hearts of those whom He sent were already His. If you want to know how they came with Him you must realize that He is from eternity. He took flesh in time, but in the beginning was the Word. . . . If He is the Truth, they who were themselves truthful came with Him . . . The times change, but not the

---

[1] Dodd, in his *Historical Tradition in the Fourth Gospel*, p. 385, claims that the thief in this parable is little more than a foil to the Shepherd. This is surely a dangerous assumption for any interpretation of the parable.

faith . . . In fellowship of faith with us are those ancients who believed that He would be born of a virgin, that He would suffer death, that He would rise and ascend to heaven", and he cites 2 Cor 4:13 and 1 Cor 10:1-3. "For them, the rock was Christ; for us, Christ is what is placed on the altar of God. They drank the water that came from the rock, foreshadowing the mystery of Christ, but we drink what the faithful know well."

Yet one cannot escape the thought that perhaps there is a glance at the official Jewish religion in the description of the hirelings. It would not be out of keeping with some of the hard things that are said in the Synoptic gospels. The point must be reserved for the chapter that will deal with the treatment of the Jews in this gospel but in the interim one may compare Jerem 23:1-2 on the shepherds who plunder and destroy the flock, and also Ezech 34:2: "Do shepherds feed themselves and not the flock:" with the warning that these shepherds will be sacked and that in the future: "I myself shall feed my sheep and they shall know that I am the Lord." One may see in Jn 10:14 that this prophecy is taken over on behalf of Christ and becomes yet another of His claims to work divine works.

Hoskyns wisely remarks (p. 366) that *Amen, Amen* in John's gospel never introduces a wholly new episode but serves to mark a step forward in the argument (5:19; 5:24-25; 6:26; 6:32; 6:47; 6:53; 8:34; 8:51; 8:58; 12:24 . . .). That being so, one must treat this parable of the Shepherd as a sequel to the episode of the man born blind. In that case the hirelings are more clearly marked out; they are those who say they have Moses for their master and cast aspersions on the parentage of Jesus (9:28-29). It is not necessary with Bernard to transfer 10:19-29 to the end of ch. 9 so that the reason

75

of the Jewish squabble of 10:19 may have an explanation. If Jesus has just (in 10:14) taken over a divine utterance and applied it to Himself there is plenty of ground for a dispute. In 10:4 there is a curious word used: "When the shepherd has *thrown out* all his own flock, he goes before them. . . ." It might mean no more than "released", but it is the word used at 2:15 for turning the sheep and oxen out of the temple and that is not usually spoken of as a release. It is also the word used for the action of the authorities in putting the man born blind out of the synagogue. Can it be that John has put it here with an overtone of meaning? When Jesus has pulled out His own from the Jewish religion, He goes before them, even to martyrdom.

"Good are the priests; but better is the high-priest who has been entrusted with the Holy of Holies, who alone has been entrusted with the hidden things of God, being Himself the door of the Father, through which have entered Abraham, Isaac and Jacob, prophets and apostles and the Church, and all of them to the unity of God." Ignatius wrote this to the Christians of Philadelphia, to whom in Apoc 3:8 John had written: "Lo, I have set before thee a door that is opened and that no one can lock."

XII

The Lamb of God

THIS title is used by John the Baptist twice in the fourth gospel, at 1:29 and 1:36. The first occasion, as we are led to understand by John's narrative in 1:32 (especially the tense of τεθέαμαι) is subsequent to the conferring of baptism on Our Lord. Now it is to be noted that in the account of this baptism in Mt 3:15 Our Lord made the mysterious remark: "Thus it becometh us to fulfil *all justice*." He cannot have been thinking of Pauline justification; the word is never used by Matthew in the Pauline sense. An acceptable sense for the word has been found (by a writer in *The Expositor* many years ago, by C. R. North and by the present writer, all working independently) by taking it to point to Isai 53:11; "The Lord was pleased to crush him with suffering. . . . Because of his soul's sorrow he shall see light; through his suffering he shall be filled. A righteous one, my servant, shall make many righteous and their iniquities he shall bear."

Here the Just One, the righteous servant, is said to be going to bear (or take up) the iniquities of all. If so, then "fulfilling all justice" could mean, to carry out to the end all that was appointed in the Prophets for the Just One, to live up to his character, even though that might involve suffering and death on behalf of sinners.

It may be felt that this interpretation credits John the Baptist with greater insight and resignation to the will of God than the apostles themselves were much later on

to give proof of, when they, and Peter in the lead, refused to accept the idea of a suffering Messias (e.g. Mt 16:22). Prat took this difficulty to heart and came to the conclusion that all that could be meant here by the word Lamb was the suggestion of innocence, the Innocent One who had not really needed to be baptized. Lagrange thought that it was not perhaps quite impossible that the Baptist should have had greater insight than the apostles, but that the difficulties of supposing this were almost insuperable. The Synoptic picture of the Baptist is of one who threatens his hearers with the Messianic wrath to come; he is one who will much later send his deputation to ask: "Art thou he who is to come?" Lagrange also urged that it was impossible to see clearly the symbolism of the Lamb as sacrificial, for the Paschal Lamb was not a sacrifice for sin, but a memorial of deliverance from Egypt, and he claimed that the idea of the Lamb as an expiatory sacrifice was first popularized by Luther.

Against this it can be urged that, as Mgr. Kissane pointed out, there is sacrificial language in Isai 53:6, which introduces the words: "He was afflicted, but he was resigned, and he opened not his mouth; like a lamb that is led to the slaughter and like a ewe that is dumb before its shearers." The action of Jahwe described in verse 6 is: "Jahwe made to light upon him the iniquities of us all", and Lev 16:21, Aaron is instructed to place his hands on the head of the scapegoat and to speak over it all the sins of the people and to place upon it, while it yet lives, all those transgressions. Isaias may be thought to be describing his lamb as sacrificial on account of this language, and if it is to this passage that the Baptist alludes, then he too will have had sacrificial overtones in his cry. Of the Fathers, Origen, Theodore

of Mopsuestia, Cyril of Alexandria, Chrysostom, Euthymius and Theophylact all think that the Baptist is designating the blood, and not merely the innocence, of the Lamb. It is true that some of these throw in for good measure the idea that the Paschal lamb is also intended by the term, and Bede and Alcuin think of the Paschal Lamb alone. Had Fr. Lagrange lived to see the recovery of the *Paschal Homily* of Melito of Sardis, he would not have put the blame for the expiatory character of the Lamb on to Luther. Melito says (44):

Once indeed the slaughter of the lamb was held in honour,
   but now in dishonour, through the life of the Lord.
Honoured was the death of the lamb, but now dishonoured,
   through the salvation of the Lord.
Honoured was the blood of the lamb, but now dishonoured,
   through the spirit of the Lord.
Honoured was the lamb that was without voice, but now
   dishonoured, through the Son who was without blame.
Honoured the temple that was below, but now dishonoured,
   through the Christ that is above.

Again in 71:

   This is the lamb that was slain:
      this is the Lamb that was without voice:
   this is he that was born of Mary the fair sheep:
      this is he that was taken from the flock,
      and was dragged to slaughter
      and was sacrificed at eventide
      and was buried in the night time,
   he that was not crushed upon the wood,
         not corrupted in the ground,
      that rose again from the dead and raiseth up mankind.

Sardis is not far from Ephesus, and if one can suppose

the oversight of the churches of Asia by John when he returned from Patmos to the mainland of Asia which is ascribed to him by some of the sources, then it is easy to see that what Melito preached at Sardis (in or about 160) could not be at variance with what John had taught at the close of the first century. Professor Van Unnik has gone further with this line of thought and claims: "The purpose of the fourth gospel was to bring the visitors of a synagogue in the Diaspora, both Jews and godfearers, to belief in Jesus as Messias of Israel." Ephesus, he says (following Ac 19:3), had those who upheld rival claims for the Baptist. It was important, then, that John should record the testimony of the Baptist that it was Jesus who was the Messias, even the suffering Messias of Isai 53. One must admit that there is some polemic in this gospel against what might be thought of as exaggerated honouring of the Baptist. It is said that he was not the light, that he did no signs, that on his own showing he was to decrease and Jesus to increase.

The late Dr. Burney put in a special plea for the linking of the Baptist's title of Lamb applied to Jesus and the Isaias passage. If the word for lamb used here was in Aramaic *taliya*, it could mean equally lamb and son. One has the feminine of this, *talitha*, at a well known place in the gospel. It is not the word used in Isai for "the servant" (*Ebed*), but that word did not carry with it (as $\pi\alpha\tilde{\iota}\varsigma$ does in Greek) the overtone of meaning that would allow it to be used for "son". If the Baptist had been enlightened by the words Our Lord said to him at the baptism about the character of the Just One, and had had a day to reflect on them, that fact in itself would be enough to account for his use now of this title "lamb". If the word used carried also a connotation of

sonship, that would be no surprise, for the voice had said: "This is My beloved Son." Certainly it is strange that John never uses ἀμνός for lamb in other parts of his writings; in the Apocalypse it is always ἀρνία. 1 Pet 1:19 and Ac 8:32 have ἀμνός, one of these passages being a direct citation of Isaias (LXX).

The lambs that Peter is told to feed are ἀρνία; the word recurs in Apoc some twenty-nine times. The symbolism is so varied that it is hard to hold it to a single pattern. In Apoc 7:17 John says that the lamb will be shepherd; he is no more bothered by the mixture of imagery than when he put together the sayings: "I am the Shepherd", and: "I am the door". The main description of the Lamb comes in Apoc 5:6–14. The seven eyes recall the Jewish imagery of Zach 3:9–10, where one may read: "The stone which I have laid before Jesus (high-priest when Zorobabel was ruler); upon one stone there are seven eyes. 'Behold I will grave the graving thereof', saith the Lord, 'and I will take away the iniquity of that land in one day'." The early Church naturally saw in this a glimpse of the Redemption, with its one day of Passion and the graving of the body of Christ by the sufferings thereof. John had anticipated them with his visions. But most of all he saw the Lamb as the centre of the adoration of all creatures (Apoc 5:13). From the surviving fragment of a Christian hymn found on papyrus we can conjecture how much this harmony of all creation was invoked in the prayer of early times: "As we sing in praise of Father, Son and Holy Spirit, may all the powers of nature join in harmony; praise and power to the sole giver of all good things; Amen: Amen." This note of cosmic harmony was strongly emphasized in the prayers that can be found cited in Firmicus Maternus (in the fourth

century) and even until the so-called Mone masses of
c. 650:

> Summe Deus semperque manens dominator ubique
> et qui cuncta potens propriis animata figuris
> artefice sermone facis, quique edita cernens
> ante videns rerumque creans per nomina formas
> cum fierent; vox semen erat, nec distulit ortus
> imperium natura sequens; mox spiritus oris
> aethera curvavit, sola nexuit, aequora fudit,
> materiamque operis sola est largita voluntas.

When the priest saying his office now comes on a phrase
about the *trina mundi machina,* he is perhaps distracted
by it but seldom recognizes that it is a survival from the
prayer of the earliest times.

The Lamb is shown (Apoc 7:17 and 22:1–3) as
synthronos, the sharer of the throne of God. This was a
recognized image used in the emperor-worship. All over
the East there had sprung up temples of Rome and
Augustus, in which the emperor was displayed to the
credulous subject-peoples as sharing the throne of a
goddess who symbolized the might of Rome. That John
should have had visions characterized by imagery of
this kind is no more surprising than that in the age
when emblems were all the fashion, Margaret Mary
should have had a vision of the heart of Christ.

XIII

The Anointed One

PHILO never used the word χριστός in all his voluminous writings; Josephus used it only when he came to speak of Jesus and his followers, and then he used it not in the sense of "the expected Messias of the Jews", for Josephus had long since ceased to believe in that prospect, but in the sense of "the one from whom the Christians get their name". At Qumran it was different, among a group where Hellenism played little or no part and where long sessions of scripture study were held regularly. But in the Dispersion, and even among the Jews of Palestine, there was little stirring of Messianic expectation before Jesus came. It is customary to balance the popular expectation of a political Messias against the teaching of Jesus that He was a suffering Messias, but this can be overdone. Until the middle of the first century there was really not much evidence of politico-religious agitation. The Egyptian who, according to Ac 21:38, had led 4,000 into the desert claimed that he would make the walls of Jerusalem fall down so that his followers might march in; this looks like emulation of Josue, but not like a Messianic claim. It may even have owed something to loose talk among Christians about "crossing the Jordan" in baptism.

The Messianic secret of the Synoptic gospels, impressed on the disciples and on witnesses of miracles in Jewish areas, but not inculcated in the Decapolis (Mk 5:19–20), is not commented on by John, but he

seems to have known about it. His account of the abrupt self-revelation of Jesus to the Samaritan woman is not followed by any comment that this was in Samaria where such teaching could safely be given, whereas in Judaea or Galilee it would have quickly precipitated such a crisis in the relations of Jesus with the authorities of state and temple that there would have been no further question of training the apostles. John might have told us all this, but did not. Instead he gives us the benefit of his reflections on the mystery of Jewish blindness (12:37–43). Here John returns over ground that had been covered by Matthew (13:14–15) and puts his own mark upon it. Isai 6:9–10 had been one of the capital texts of the early preaching. It is Paul's last word to the Jews of Rome (Ac 28:26) when they refuse to hear him further, though elsewhere (Rom 11:25) Paul will say that the *sclerosis* in Israel is only partial, until the plenitude of the Gentiles has come in. John has taken the Pauline (and Marcan) metaphor of hardening by the action of water (forming stalactites) or by the formation of a callosity, in place of the LXX rendering of the text, where the word used is simply that for the heaviness that comes of running to fat. It may not be fanciful to see in this a consequence of apostolic preaching as the time drew on and the Jews still stayed outside the Church. Fatness is a common failing, not quite natural, but none the less frequent, whereas the disease of the stone is not in any sense natural. John is not here reporting a discourse of Our Lord but giving his own thoughts. He has brought into relation with the well-used text from Isai 6 another, from the beginning of the Suffering Servant prophecy of Isai 53: "Who has believed our showing?" It would seem then that he thinks of the stony negative response of Israel as part of

the suffering of Christ and as already indicated in the prophecy. As Fr. Martindale so well comments: "If grace be constantly resisted, men become unable to accept God's revelation." It is not merely a question of "petrifying the feeling", but of dulling the mind and will.

In the light of the maxim *Habenti dabitur*, John's own teaching about the anointing that all Christ's flock have received becomes clearer. In his first Epistle (2:20–27) he proclaims: "You have an anointing from the Holy One and you all know it." It must therefore have been part of the ordinary catechesis at that time to explain what this anointing was, and who it was from. John himself calls Jesus the holy One (6:69 and Apoc 3:7), but uses the title for the Father (17:11 and Apoc 4:8; 6:10) also. It must suffice us to leave his language in this uncertainty, knowing as we do that anointing is attributed elsewhere to the Spirit and the Spirit proceeds from both Father and Son. John had no need to be more precise.

The Valentinian *Gospel of Truth* has so much about anointing that it has been claimed by a Swedish critic as a confirmation-homily. At 36:18 it says: "The anointing is the mercy of the Father, with which He will have mercy on them. And those whom He has anointed are complete. For it is the full jars that are wont to be anointed. But when the anointing of one jar shall be destroyed, it is wont to leak. And the reason why it shall lack content is the fact that its anointing shall depart from it. For at that time a breath is wont to draw it, a breath marked by the power of that which is with it. But with Him who is without lack, the seal of none is wont to be cast off before Him, nor is any wont to leak. But what he lacks, He is wont to fill up for him—He,

85

the Father, who is perfect." After that one may be happy to return to John's more simple utterance in his Epistle. In 2:24 he recalls the faithful to what they have learnt "from the beginning"; some think this could cover their readings in the OT when they still frequented the synagogue, but it clearly means their catechesis, whatever else it may include. This catechesis was the preaching of Jesus (it is Paul who calls Jesus the first Apostle, but John needs only to imply it) and its sum is eternal life.

In the same Epistle (2:26–27) John speaks of the anointing as coming from the Anointed One, for it is clearly Christ who "taught you to abide in Him". How this anointing dispenses with the need for a teacher is very obscure. If the anointing is the light of divine faith infused into the soul, then even a theologian would admit that such light brings with it what he would call a supernatural knowledge of spiritual things comparable to the connatural knowledge which the mind has by sympathy with its object. St. Thomas (*Summa* 2–2ae: 1:4:43 and 45:2:c) calls it *lumen fidei* and says that one who has the habitual disposition to be chaste has a right judgment about chastity, even though he may not know moral science well; and even so there is a "connatural" knowledge of divine things, by gift of the Holy Spirit. An habitual set of the will and an affective disposition towards the objects of the faith will enable a man to discern between true and false devotions or doctrines when newly presented to him, even though he be no great theologian. This kind of knowledge is sponsored in the encyclical *Humani Generis* (D 2324) and may well stand for what John here meant. He seems to promise something like it in 6:45. He could also have in mind that his faithful did not need NEW teachers

after they had once been taught the faith and hence they should be wary of the Gnostics, but that is left in the background.

For those who are outside the Messianic secret (for whom, as the synoptics would say, there are only parables) John is concerned in 10:24 and 12:34. In the first incident, at Hanukkah (the feast of Lights) in the temple, the question is put plainly: "Are you the Christ?" Whatever the term meant to the crowd (and one is not bound to suppose they had their cue from the discourse about the Good Shepherd and its relation to Ezechiel 34), the answer Jesus gives is that, if they were obedient to the prompting of grace (if they were of His sheep), then they would be enabled to believe fully in His teaching. They have gone through the preambles of faith as far as reasoning will take them, for, as they say themselves, their souls are "up in the air", held in suspense. This must mean that their curiosity has been so far aroused as to make them think this man is credible, and is worth listening to; but, instead of being ready to believe now, they want sight, or a plain declaration that would force their assent. That they cannot have, and they will not become His sheep. Jesus describes Himself as the one whom the Father sanctified and sent into the world, thus coming near enough to a plain but not over-mastering declaration, and their reaction is to take up stones to the blasphemer. As Hoskyns points out, the LXX makes a distinction (not present in the Hebrew) between the dedication of things and the sanctification of men; the temple is dedicated (10:22), but Jesus is sanctified (10:36 and 17:17).

The interrogation reported at 12:34 is of great moment, for it shows that by now the crowd has understood the identification of the Christ and the Son of

Man. It is in terms of this "son-of-man Christology" that they put their difficulty, for it is Dan 7:13–14 that suggests the permanence for ever of the Christ in that character. "The glory of the Messias will never fail", said Enoch (1:41), and the Messianic psalm 109 had the word about "a priest for ever", but it is chiefly Daniel with his promise of eternal power for the Son of Man who is in question here.

XIV

The Revelation of the Father

IT is hard for a Jew to accept that Jesus was both God and man. There are some Jews who say they accept that Jesus was their Messias but cannot bring themselves to believe what is in the Nicene Creed. A recent book by a Rabbinical scholar on the history of the Sanhedrin offers considerable evidence of the fact that it was no blasphemy for a Jew to claim to be Messias and then concludes that therefore the gospel accounts of the trial of Jesus must be wrong; the alternative, that His claim was not only to Messiahship but to the divine nature, is not envisaged. In the early preaching it was obviously necessary to approach the mystery of the Incarnation gradually, Jesus being first presented to inquirers as Messias, and then, if they engaged themselves to become catechumens, they were taught the whole truth and enabled to confess at their baptism that Christ is God. Of the few passages in Paul's letters where Jesus is called God (Rom 9:5 and Tit 2:13, with possibly Hebr 1:8) a Non-conformist writer (A. Wainwright, *The Trinity in the N.T.*) remarks: "Paul allowed himself to write down what he was ready to say in the intensity of worship but was in the habit of restraining himself from writing in his letters." John has a Jewish *inclusio* framing his gospel and thus bringing forward the truth of Jesus's claim, the opening verse (1:1) being answered by the proclamation by Thomas at 20:28, so that the whole narrative of the gospel is given this truth as its keynote, like some festal psalm with its antiphon.

89

Where the technical terms of nature and person are yet undeveloped, it is necessary to state that the equality with the Father that Jesus claimed was not an "all-round" equality. Hence one could expect that there would be passages in John's work that would bring this out. In 8:28 there is one of the "I am" sayings (see below) which sets forth a claim to equality with God and immediately there is added the qualification that in fact the Son uses no initiative in His work but reveals to men just what the Father has laid down. The statement was one of fact, not of right, but the Jewish audience could be expected to take it as an admission of subordination of some kind. Theologians of later times might understand it to embody the truth that all the works of the Trinity in regard to creatures are works done in common by all three Persons, but the language used in the text would look like that of subordination, were it not for the absence of any adversative particle between the two statements. Chrysostom seems to have caught the drift exactly when he says (*hom.* 53 in Jn) that the saying nothing of Himself indicates the indistinguishability of substance between Son and Father, whereas the events that are hinted at in the words about "lifting up" will show the Jews that Jesus has divine power, when they see His resurrection and His conquest. Barrett comments: "John cannot mean that the Jews will recognize the truth of Jesus's claims after the Crucifixion, since it was well known to him that this had not happened." This is a fair comment only if one supposes that John is writing the speeches of Jesus with complete hindsight. It is to be noted that Jesus does not say: "You will believe", but, "you will know", meaning that they will have the arguments of credibility set before them with such

clarity that a plea of ignorance will no longer be possible.

The words in 10:18 about willingness to die and the command of the Father are roughly parallel to the text just considered. Jesus states that He lays down His life of Himself, of His own free motion, and yet He adds that He has received a command from the Father so to do. The order of the two statements is not without significance; first His own choice and then the command of the Father, so that we may understand that once again it is not a question of subordination in nature between the Persons but of what we have to describe as a common choice of the Three which in its object concerns primarily one of them for its execution. Jesus's claim that He lays down His life freely has been borne out by events that have already happened at the time of speaking; 8:59 is one occasion where Jesus escaped stoning by His own power, quite apart from the episode of Nazareth recounted by Luke (4:29–30). The strange happening at the arrest, recounted by John alone (18:6), where once more Jesus uses the words "I am", is again an indication of the free surrender of Himself to which the present claim alludes, while the loud cry from the cross (in all the Synoptics, but not in John) might be taken in the same sense, for no dying man after so much suffering would have the strength to raise his voice.

In 10:36 Jesus describes Himself as the one whom the Father hallowed and sent into the world. This hallowing is simply a setting apart for God's service, and should not be understood in the sense that Jesus had somehow to be brought up to a standard of holiness that He did not previously reach. Jesus could have settled His argument with the Jews at this point by an

a fortiori: "If the Scripture could call certain creatures Gods, and Sons of the most High, without blasphemy, how much more proper is it that I should use that title, when I have equality of nature with the Father?" But he does not go about to shock them in that way. Rather, He takes the humble line of argument, appealing to His divine mission first, and then to the works that give it credibility and make apparent the soundness of the claim to equality. There is also another reason for this line being followed here. In 17:17–19 Jesus is to pray that in their turn His disciples may be hallowed, or set apart in the truth, even as He was. Here John is deepening the familiar teaching found in the Synoptics that, "he who receiveth you receiveth Me" (Mt 10:40 etc.). John knew this (13:17–20), in its Matthean form, and appealed to it on another occasion too (12:44–45). He cannot be thought to be innovating on his own account in this deepening of the saying, for the circumstances of the final discourse are such that they make it most suitable for Christ to go as far in His language to the apostles then as He ever intended to go.

In His sacerdotal prayer Christ asks not only for the hallowing of His disciples but declares: "For them I hallow myself". These words are difficult. "I set myself apart for My divinely appointed task", is an adequate paraphrase, though Chrysostom says it means simply: "I make myself a sacrifice", and is a hint of what is to come in the Passion. If so, what is to be made of the use of the same word for the disciples? Are they to be made a sacrifice according to the latter part of 17:19: "That they may be sacrificed in truth?" In 17:11 Jesus asked that they might be kept safe; it would be strange if here He prayed for their martyrdom. Yet not so strange. If the keeping safe meant that they were to be

kept safe in doctrine, then the witnessing to that doctrine could easily involve them in martyrdom. Chrysostom is willing to keep this sense in both parts of the verse and suggests that possibly the intent is that they may be joined to the sacrifice of their Head. This interpretation would best explain the extension of the prayer to the Church as a whole in verse 20. The essential ambiguity of John's term "glory" supports this view, for suffering and triumph are both parts of that notion as they are of this "sanctification" or setting apart.

The hallowing that Jesus asks of the Father in 17:19 is what He Himself claims to give in 15:3 and what He says the Spirit will provide in 16:13, and this is a characteristic way for John to indicate the equality of the Three Persons. He has similar overlappings elsewhere, cf. what was said about "the Holy One" in 1 Jn 2:20. He does not need to cite a triple formula where the three Names are put side by side, as in Mt 28:20 but the reality of Trinitarian worship is his.

The "I am" sayings (the Hebrew for which is *Ani hu*, cf. Isai 43:10) are not strictly grammatical in Greek, and 8:24 in particular seems to leave the hearers expecting the sentence to be continued. That may be Johannine irony, for the Jewish audience are given a bigger shock when the phrase is repeated in 8:58; then they understand the claim to a title parallel to that used by Jahwe in Exod 3:14–16 and take up stones to stop the blasphemy. John is not innovating by the use of this phrase, since it is recorded, in both Mt 14:27 and Mk 6:50, that it was with this same phrase that Jesus greeted them as He walked on the water. It occurs again in Jn at 6:20 and 18:6, while 13:29 has it in a context that implies that its use was habitual. Often in John do

93

we meet with the phrase completed by a title: "I am the Door" etc., and it may be that this habit was cultivated by Jesus to make the disciples familiar with His claim thus to take over one of the attributes of Jahwe.

If 14:7 contains a reproach ("If you had known Me, as you do not, then you would have known My Father"), one can understand the interruption by Philip much better, but not all the codices support such a version. *Sinaiticus* and *codex Bezae* with the Bodmer papyrus are in favour of an open future condition, not an unfulfilled one from the past. Then the sense is that, as they now know Jesus, they will go on to know the Father. The Jews had the endemic fear of death from the sight of God (Exod 33:18 etc.) and the disciples must have shared this. It would be considerate of Jesus to set their minds at rest.

XV

The Paraclete

THE *Manual of Discipline* from Qumran (p. 53)
tells of the Angel of Darkness that, "all the spirits
that attend upon him are bent on causing the
sons of light to stumble. Howbeit, the God of Israel and
the Angel of His truth are always there to help the
sons of light." This idea of a helper on high who was
not God Himself was quite familiar to the Jews. They
had Job 16:19 to start with: "My witness, behold he is
in heaven and the one that is privy to my secrets is on
high." They had the word *Paraclete* taken over from
Greek and already current before the time of Our Lord
(*Pirke Aboth*, 4:11a). The word was simply spelt out in
Hebrew letters (פְּרַקְלִיט) as it was spoken in Greek, and
not translated. In the Two Ways, that catechesis of
popular morality that is common to the *Manual of
Discipline*, to the *Didache* and the *Epistle of Barnabas*, there
is (in the last two documents, at least) a use of the word
when it is said of the evil liver that he is a paraclete of
the rich and a lawless judge of the poor. St. John had
therefore no need to improvise here or to attribute to
Our Lord language which had been borrowed from
some Hellenistic philosopher; everyone knew the word
that was freely used in common speech (see also TB
Shabbat 32 a, and *Baba Bathra* 10 a).

For the meaning of the word one cannot do better
than take the now famous passage in the sermon by
G. M. Hopkins: "Often it is translated Comforter, but
a Paraclete does more than comfort. The word is

Greek; there is no one English word for it and no one Latin word. Comforter is not enough. A Paraclete is one who comforts, who cheers, who encourages, who persuades, who exhorts, who stirs up, who urges forward, who calls on; what the spur and the word of command is to a horse, what clapping of hands is to a speaker, what a trumpet is to the soldier, that a Paraclete is to the soul; one who calls us on, that is what it means; a Paraclete is one who calls us on to good." You will notice in this account that Fr. Hopkins stresses the active sense of the word; he does not bother about the passive sense of "one who is called up by us", of an intercessor who is invoked or called in to give us advice. Ignatius (Rom 7:2) has exactly this understanding of the activity of the Spirit as Paraclete when he cries out: "There is in me no fire that loveth destruction, but living water that speaketh within me and saith within me: 'Hither, towards the Father'." Now it is just this sense which fits the use of the word in 1 Jn 2:1: "If any man sin, we have one who calls us on towards the Father, Jesus Christ the just one." The preposition πρός implies motion towards, and so the usual version: "We have an advocate at the Father's side", or the like, will not quite fit the Greek, though the Latin Vulgate's *advocatum apud Patrem* bears this interpretation. John is not thinking of an exceptional case when Jesus may be thought to go to the Father and intercede for the culprit, for he has just stressed the universal fact of sin. He seems to be saying: "In spite of our sin, Christ as Paraclete calls us on to the Father, for He has Himself the wherewithal to justify us and He would not have us fall away and turn aside."

The mysterious saying at 3:34: "The one whom God hath sent speaketh the words of God; for He giveth the

Spirit and that not in niggardly fashion", should be taken to refer to Christ Himself, if one takes into account what is said at 6:63-4 and 7:39. So Cyril of Alexandria (PG 73:280) took the place, before any opposition in the Greek church had developed to the idea of the Spirit proceeding from the Son. *Codex Bezae* however, with some other Greek MSS., with the Syriac and Coptic versions and Origen, has supplied ὁ θεός (God) as subject to this sentence, and some of these even specify "God the Father". Origen cannot be suspected of secret dislike of the *Filioque*, but some of the versions can. If the Spirit is a caller-on, then one can see a causal connection between the two statements. In effect, Christ is God's messenger to us and He is not niggardly in giving the Spirit, who calls us on, or comforts us, through the words of God that are spoken by Christ. In 1:32 John the Baptist has been reported as saying that the Spirit "was abiding upon Jesus" after the baptism, i.e., the descent which is chronicled in the Synoptics was to be understood as no mere passing accident but as a permanent condition. Thus from possession of the Spirit to the giving thereof is a natural development.

The bestowal of the Spirit by Jesus in 20:22 is marked with greater solemnity, for the description involves the use of the ritual act of breathing upon the disciples, an act borrowed from the Jewish creation story of Gn 2:7. (The word ʾεμφυσῶ, with Hebrew נָפַח, is found nowhere else in the Bible except Ezech 37:9, the field of bones, and Wis 15:11, which repeats the idea of Genesis.) The Church in her liturgy has accepted this attribution of function and proclaims (*Secret* for Whit Tuesday) that the Holy Spirit is Himself the forgiveness of sins. The metaphor of "loosing and retaining" that is used here is a taxation-term. The sinner is "spoken free"

of his debt or alternatively the debt is insisted upon or retained; the speaking-free can obviously be the work of the One who calls us on and comforts us, and it is by that principally, rather than by His retaining of sins, that He is named. One may notice that John has reinterpreted the older and more Jewish metaphor used in the promise to Peter (Mt 16:18) and to the apostles (Mt 18:18), which was of a power similar to that of imposing or relaxing the synagogue-ban and of allowing or forbidding a doctrine[1] (for the Jews did not sharply and legalistically distinguish teaching authority and disciplinary). This shift of emphasis made apparent by the change of metaphors may be a sign of the growing-up of the Church and of her moving away from Jewish surroundings. It is perhaps significant that before a pagan was baptized in the early Church "for the remission of his sins" he went through a renunciation of the world which was called by another taxation-word: *apotaxis*. The word first appears in *Hermas*.

The difficulty is made (e.g. by Barrett, p. 475) that this giving of the Spirit is not compatible with the Lucan account, where the Spirit is to be awaited after the Ascension (Lk 24:48 and Ac 1:4) and is then given on Pentecost (Ac 2). But this is to misunderstand the piecemeal way of Jewish narrative. John's tale of the breathing and Luke's of the boisterous wind are not exclusive of each other. There is a gestation-period for the given Spirit, in the fifty days from Easter to Pentecost, or, if one prefer it, a distinction between having and using. The early Church found no difficulty in the separation of the blessing of the apostles by Christ's imposed hands at His Ascension (Lk 24:50) from the coming of the Spirit; both were parts of one act and

[1] The doctrinal power is given in Jn 20:21.

originally they were commemorated on the one day of Pentecost, but gradually the chronology of Luke prevailed with its mention of forty days from Easter to Ascension.

The Paraclete sayings of 14:26 onwards are a great stumbling-block to the critics, for they speak of the Spirit as a Person beyond any doubt. If John had wanted to avoid this implication, he could have continued to use the neuter word *pneuma* for Spirit, but, on the contrary, Jesus even uses the personal pronoun "that one" (ἐκεῖνος) for the Paraclete in 16:12 and puts Himself on a footing with the Paraclete in 14:16 by calling Him *another*, or a second, Paraclete. John does not elaborate a proof of the divinity of the Spirit as he does for Jesus, since that was not the scope of his gospel. One may guess that he saw in the coming life of the Church the ground on which that proof would be based; there would have to be the claims to possess the Spirit, and the miracles in support to make those claims credible (which is as far as the proof has to go), but all the Fathers look on their own time as the age of the Spirit; the OT period being that of the Father, and the years of Christ being that of the Son.

There is a passage in Hermas (*Mand* 10:3) about the work of the Paraclete. "The sour man is ever doing ill. The first ill he does is to grieve the Holy Spirit who is given to men as a source of cheerfulness. Then, grieving the Holy Spirit, he doth iniquity by not praying nor confessing to the Lord. For the prayer of the sour man hath not the power to rise up to God's altar of sacrifice. Why does the prayer of the sour man not rise up to the altar? Because his heart is settled in sourness. Sourness is mixed with his prayer and will not let it go cleanly to the altar. For as sour wine and sweet when mixed

together do not give the same pleasure, so sourness mixed with the Holy Spirit hath not the same power of intercession." Origen (*de orat* 10:2) says much the same of the Son as Paraclete: The high priest of our offerings and Paraclete to the Father is the Son, beseeching for those who beseech and joining with the intercessors in their intercession." It is this active "Paracleting" that is given in Ac 9:3 1; 15:31.

The idea of the Spirit as an accuser is not absent from John 16:8–11. The Son had come for judgment (9:39), and the Spirit continues His work. Judgment has begun from "the Prince of this world" (12:31), and in a sense it is going on all the time. Perhaps that is how the Spirit is to tell us of what is going to happen (16:13), by showing it as already under way. The world cannot receive the Spirit (14:17) and, as this incompatibility becomes manifest, the judgment of the world is made plain, at least to those who believe. In 15:26 the Spirit is said to be going to witness for Jesus. This "appearance for the defence" is also an accusation against the wilfully blind. "Who shall be our Paraclete, if we are found not to have works that are holy and just?" asks 2 Clem 6:9.

XVI

John's Doctrine of *Agape*

BY the time John wrote, the celebration of the *Agape* was an established custom. Soon Ignatius would be calling the church at Rome: "the one that presides over the *Agape* of Christians", and the existence of this solemn supper after the Eucharist must be presumed for Ephesus in John's time. Everything, therefore, that Our Lord had said about love, where this word was used, would have overtones for the audience for whom John first wrote. Thus 1 Jn 3:11 refers the commandment to have *Agape* one with another to that period of time which John in several places designates as "the beginning". It is as if he says: "You may think that our practice of the love-feast is a recent development, but you should know that from the beginning Christ commanded us to show love to each other as here we are trying to do." In 15:27 and 16:4 (and possibly in 6:64) "the beginning" means the time when the disciples began receiving their instructions from Our Lord, but sometimes (as in 8:44; 1 Jn 3:8) it looks back to the very beginning of time. "From the beginning" is thus one of those Johannine ambiguities which he sometimes resorts to in the effort to transmit his high doctrine. There is a pattern about the history of salvation which Paul has already declared by making Christ the second Adam and which Irenaeus would later describe as ἀνακεφαλαίωσις: *recirculatio* (adv. haer. 3:32:1); John is content to imply it by this ambiguous phrase which (in 8:44) points back to the story in Genesis, as do the words of

19:26 (where the word *Woman* is a direct appeal to Gen 3:15) and 19:28, by which John indicates his belief in the existence of just such a divine plan of *recirculatio*.

In the discussion of *Agape* in 1 Jn 2:7–10 a further paradox is introduced. Though the command to love each other has been from the beginning, it is in some sense a new command. What that sense is may be gathered from the phrase in verse 8 about the darkness passing away and the genuine light beginning to appear. It is as if John said: "I am not one of those who think that the illumination of baptism is enough for men without anything more. Unless baptized persons go on to practise this *Agape*, they might as well stay in darkness. The one who does practise it has not only come to the light but abides in it." This is the force of verse 9, and this is exactly what St. Augustine understands by the passage. In his *tract.* 1 on John's epistles he says: "Here is someone who was a pagan. He has become a Christian. Now understand me; when he was a pagan he was in darkness. Now he has become a Christian, everyone is glad. *Deo gratias.* We have that place from St. Paul read (Eph 5:8) about once being darkness and now light in the Lord. He adored idols; now he adores God. He adored what he had made; now he adores one who made him. He is changed, thanks be to God, and all Christians are glad. He has become the adorer of Father, Son and Holy Ghost, and a hater of demons and idols. But John is still bothered about this man. While many are showing their joy, he is concerned. Let us, brethren, accept the concern of our mother. For not without reason is she concerned about us while others rejoice; I mean our mother, charity. For charity was in the heart of John when he said these things. . . . If you hold fast to charity, you will not suffer scandal, neither

over Christ nor His Church. The man who is scandalized over Christ is like one scorched by the sun; if over
the Church, like one scorched by the moon. Does not
the psalm say: 'The sun will not scorch thee by day nor
the moon by night'? . . . A man who is being scorched
says: 'I can't bear it. I won't stand it', and he goes out.
Now that is what some do who fall away on account
of Christ or the Church."

But what of the paradox of 13:34, where the command to have *Agape* is called new, whereas (as Chrysostom says) it could be found even in the OT (or in
Pirke Aboth 1:12: where Hillel said: "Be disciples of
Aaron . . ., loving mankind and bringing them nigh to
the Law".)? The answer is that the manner is new,
not the substance. For Christ there adds: "as I have
loved you". If we take it that the institution of the
Eucharist took place just before these words were spoken
(and Tatian inserted the institution-narrative from the
Synoptics at 13:32 in his harmony of the gospels), then
the manner in which Christ showed His love is plain.
The suggestion of Dr. Barrett: "The immediate reference is to the feet-washing (verse 14)", is not one that
is likely to win general acceptance. He is on firmer
ground when he says: "The mutual love of Christian
disciples is different from any other; it is modelled
upon, and in some measure reveals, the mutual love of
the Father and the Son". This brings us to what the
theologians have called the analogy of love. Just as the
term "being" is applied by analogous predication to God
and to creatures, so the term "love", and hence there
is to be observed a similarity and a difference between
divine mutual love within the Trinity and human.
Richard of St. Victor thought he had an acceptable
argument of reason for the existence of the Trinity of

persons in God when he urged that among creatures the mutual love of two is not satisfied unless one of them (or both) have a confidant, who is not the loved one but to whom the joy of this love can be communicated. One might reply that he was transposing to the divine sphere an aspect of human love which all too obviously belonged to its human limitations. It is only when these limitations of human love have been removed in thought that the analogy can be strictly applied. 1 Jn 1:3 is authority for saying that John himself clearly understood the truth of this analogy of love, but the term of *koinonia* which he there uses will be considered in the next chapter. In the gospel (15:9) there is the revelation of the analogy by Christ Himself. "As the Father has loved Me, so I also . . ." The love of the Father for the Son has been the theme of earlier sayings of Jesus (3:35; 5:20; 10:17) but in each of these the added words are concerned with the works of Jesus, His miracles, or His saving death; it is only now, and in the context of the Eucharist, that the analogy of love is proclaimed.

The polemic with the Jews in 5:41–44, in which they are accused of not having *Agape*, shows the negative side of the teaching on love. It is because the Jews are preoccupied in seeking glory from each other (7:18; 12:43) that they are incapable of *Agape*. "I seek not glorification from men (but you do), and I have come to know that you have not the *Agape* of God in you. I have come in the name of My Father and you do not accept Me; another will come in his own name and him you will accept." That the title "only-begotten Son" was synonymous with "beloved Son" was commonly accepted by the Fathers of the Church (see C. H. Turner, JTS [1925] 113–29). It can be seen from the parable of the

Wicked Husbandmen (Mk 12:6 and Lk 20:13, though not Mt 21:37) that this identification was natural. Mark even suggests it by his wording: "Yet had he one, a beloved son." It is not to be wondered at, therefore, if Jesus, in this polemic with the Jews, allows His thoughts to run back to the Father's love for the Son and how that love might come to abide in men. The normal way of this love working itself out is a descent, from the Father through the Son, to men and from men to one another; so 17:23, 26. But there is the idea of a return of *Agape* to the Son from men. In fact (3:19) many of them have loved darkness rather than light, and (8:42) if, as they claimed, God was really their father, they would seek to return His love through the Son, but instead they follow the lusts of their father the devil. It does not seem wrong to notice a subtle change of language here in John; he will not speak of their having *Agape* for their master the devil, but simply that they follow his *epithumiai* or lusts.

The priority is God's in the descent of *Agape*; that is the message of 1 Jn 4:7–8, though the Vulgate at 1 Jn 4:10 has interpolated the word *prior* to fill out the obvious sense of the passage. John never uses this divine attribute of *Agape* (which he has here made the definition of God) to describe the Son, as he does the attributes of life (1 Jn 5:20) and light (1 Jn 1:5). Perhaps he felt that it should be more properly reserved for the Spirit of God. Yet John will not let this priority of *Agape* turn into a cold-blooded system of predestination. There is (1 Jn 2:29) emphasis on human activity; he who does justice is born of God, and (1 Jn 3:7, 10) is just, even as Jesus was just. In 1 Jn 5:1 belief and birth from God are linked together, and as yet no priority is marked between them. That would come later. In Didymus of

Alexandria there is a comment on the text of Isaias: "Come ye to the waters; buy without money wine and milk" (55:1). "The water means baptism and the wine and milk the participation of the Body and Blood of Christ, and this we do indeed buy at our regeneration, paying out faith and not silver, and yet at the same time we receive a free gift" (PG 39:716). John had left the same two positions side by side in the Jewish manner, for, after the text about human activity in 1 Jn 2:29, he immediately adds in 3:1 that God gives us the great gift of *Agape*.

The connection of love and sight was familiar in the ancient theory of vision. Seeing assimilates, and likeness is the cause of love. That is what 1 Jn 3:2 seems to be saying, but the text needs repunctuation, thus: "We are now the children of God, and He has not yet been made manifest. What we shall be, we know, for, if He be made manifest, we shall be like Him, for we shall see Him as He is." The verb φανερῶ is never used impersonally in John; and see especially 1 Jn 2:28, which is a close parallel to this place.

XVII

Koinonia: Fellowship in the Church

SHARING between friends was among the Greeks
erected into a philosophical principle. They had
a proverb about friends having all in common,
but from their mathematical studies the Platonists came
to see that there was a principle of nature behind this
proverb. They had discovered the existence of friendly
numbers, the first pair being 220 and 284. The property
of these numbers was that, if all the factors of one
number were taken and added together, the sum was
the other number, and then its factors, if taken and
added together, would give the first number. Thus
$10 + 22 + 11 + 20 + 110 + 2 + 5 + 44 + 4 + 55 + 1$
$= 284$, and $4 + 71 + 2 + 142 + 1 = 220$. Plato had
postulated some kind of friendliness between his ideas
or forms in their lofty region apart, and later philo-
sophers such as Philo used the idea of sharing or friendliness even for the relations of God to man. He says (*vita
Moysis* 1:158) that man enjoys a *koinonia* or sharing with
the Father of all things under certain conditions, and he
applies the same idea to the sacrificing priests in the
temple (*de spec. legibus* 1:131): "They become sharers
of what is given in thank-offering to God," and later in
the same work (1:221) God is described as "sharer of
the altar and table-companion".

Now in 1 Jn 1:3–7 the noun *koinonia* is used four times
and in 2 Jn 11 the verb is used, but nowhere in the
gospel is there a trace of either. Is this, then, an instance
of John taking over a philosophical idea from the

THE THEOLOGY OF ST. JOHN

Greeks which he did not find in the traditional Jewish-Christian teaching? Certainly he employs the word to denote a relationship between Christians and at the same time with the Father and the Son, while the second Epistle has the counterpart, of fellowship with evil, to set off that with the good. One may begin by testing the possibility that John had picked up the word from Paul, for the whole nest of ideas connected with the word is already to be found in Paul's epistles. In 1 Cor 1:9 he speaks of our fellowship with Jesus through the calling of the Father, while the eucharistic passage of the same epistle (1 Cor 10:16) speaks of fellowship in the Body and Blood of Christ, this phrase showing how the two fellowships come to be linked together, for, if there is a sharing of the individual Christian with the Father and the Son, this is not a thing that happens in private seclusion but in the public liturgy of the Church, and hence what we enjoy each towards God is somehow extended to become a relationship between Christians who worship together. These are ideas that do not appear in Philo; he had no idea of such eucharistic communion, for, when he spoke of the priests communicating with God, it was by means of the thank-offering sacrifices which God allowed them to share with Himself. Again there is in Paul (2 Cor 6:14–18) a most illuminating passage on fellowship with light or with darkness that corresponds to what John has in his second Epistle.

With Paul we seem to be going back to primitive Christian thought, for in the passage last cited he has a most interesting fusion of OT texts, which is a mark of the primitive church-teaching, when such combination of proof texts took place freely. Isai 52:11 has been fused with Ezech 20:34 and 41, with some help from Jer 51:45 and then continued with 2 Sam 7:14 (a very

popular early Christian text), not without a word or two being supplied for which there is no warrant in the OT at all. The background of this fusion may lie in a passage of Malachy (2:10–16) which I cite in the Douay version: "Why is there not one Father of us all? Hath not one God created us? Why then doth everyone of us despise his brother, violating the covenant of our fathers? Juda hath transgressed and abomination was done in Israel and in Jerusalem; because Juda hath contaminated the sanctification of the Lord, which he loved, and hath had the daughter of a strange god. The Lord will destroy the man that hath done this; the master and the scholar out of the tabernacles of Jacob, and him that offereth gifts to the Lord of hosts. And this again have you done; you covered the altar of the Lord with tears, with weeping and howling, so that I have respect no more for sacrifice, neither do I accept any placable thing at your hands. And you have said: 'For what cause?' Because the Lord hath testified between thee and the wife of thy youth, whom thou hast despised, and she thy partaker and the wife of thy covenant . . ."

One can see how the early Christians would take this to themselves for its seeming description of Judas Iscariot, and all the more after the cessation of the temple sacrifices in 69. The nuptial imagery, too, indicates another way in which fellowship between Christians was understood. Such imagery is frequent in the OT to describe the relation of Jahwe and Israel, and Our Lord had given it a new sense when he spoke of Himself as the Bridegroom (Mt 9:15; Mk 2:19, and in Jn 3:29, from the Baptist). The idea of the Christian body as a close fellowship, cut off from Jewry as well as from the Gentiles to make a third race, is well known

to the Apologists and must have been in practice almost forced upon the early Church. The call to "come out from wickedness" must have been often repeated. It is not by chance that we hear it in Apoc 18:4: "I heard another voice from heaven saying: 'Go out from her, my people, that you be not partakers of her sins and receive not of her plagues; because her sins are come even to heaven and God hath remembered her iniquities. Render to her as she also hath rendered to you, and double ye double according to her works. In the cup wherein she hath mingled, mingle ye double unto her. As much as she hath glorified herself and hath been in delicacies; so much give her torment and mourning; because she saith in her heart: "I sit a queen, and widow I am not, and mourning I shall not see." Therefore in one day shall her plagues come, death and mourning and famine, and with fire shall she be burnt, because God is strong that shall judge her.' " "Coming out from wickedness", being bound to God in eucharistic fellowship and the fulfilment of the Ezechiel prophecy that God would make his dwelling with them (Ezech 37:27) through a *kataskenosis* much greater than the Shekinah of the past; all this would easily combine in the Christian mind, as it did in Paul's quotation. From this one may derive a clue to explain the absence of this language from John's gospel. He is there reporting objectively, without allowing later language to colour his expressions, and he keeps strictly to the terms Christ had used Himself about "remaining with you" or "abiding in you", while not trying to restate them in terms of "fellowship". God abides in Christ (14:10) and Christ (14:27) has been abiding with them. Now (15:4–10) in His parable of vine and branches He appeals to them to abide in Him. The Jews are said

(5:38) not to have the word of God abiding in them, while in 6:56 it is by eating the flesh of the Son of Man that they are to abide in Him. When he comes to his own letters, John can continue this language (1 Jn 3:6, 24; 4:16), while adding to it the later language of *koinonia*.

In Ac 2:42 the "teaching of the apostles" and "the fellowship" are paired off against "the breaking of bread" and "the prayers." (Note that the Vulgate has destroyed this pairing by a wrong translation.) The first and last terms are fairly clear, but what are fellowship and breaking of bread? It is commonly thought that to break bread was to celebrate the Eucharist, but that cannot be proved. Seven times in the Synoptics, and also in Jn 6:12–13, the broken fragments of the multiplied loaves are called *klasmata*, and in 1 Cor 10:16 the bread we break is admitted by all to be the Eucharist. But what was Paul doing in Ac 27:35, when he took bread on board ship after the storm? The D-text has tried to make Paul's act into a eucharist by adding the words "distributing to us also" after the word *ate*; but neither the giving of thanks nor the ceremonial breaking forces us to accept that this was in fact a eucharistic act. Further, in verse 34, Paul has called on the crew to take food and in verse 36 they do so after his example; it is hard then to suppose that this was the Eucharist. But, if not here, then the eucharistic sense of "breaking bread" cannot be enforced elsewhere. To return to the word "fellowship", it has been argued that it means something like "membership of the Church", a term for this being at first lacking. Other meanings suggested are "companionship of the apostles", as in Gal 2:9, or else "almsgiving", with reference to what is said in 2:44 about the holding of all things in common. By the time John came to write his letters that experiment in

communal living had come to an end and he could not have had this in mind. One is left, then, with the idea that "fellowship" is something that starts among the apostles, to whom others are joined as they come to be baptized.

In 11:16 John has used a word that is found nowhere else in the NT, yet it has become a common term among modern writers, the word "fellow-disciples". "Thomas said to his fellow-disciples: 'Let us go and join with Him in death'." From what we have seen earlier about the value John sets on the collective witness of the Twelve, it should not be hard to see what this term means. The Twelve stand together: "We know that his testimony is true: we must take up our cross and follow Him. If Peter is to be bound and led off to death, what is to happen to John? Will he not be somehow involved in the same fate?" If he is John, "your brother and partaker in tribulation and the kingdom and patience in Christ Jesus" (Apoc 1:9), why should he not be?

This term "partaker" is an interesting exception to the usual practice in John, who avoids almost of set purpose the many coinings of compound terms made by Paul with the help of the prefix *syn-*. They must have been common Christian language at the time John was writing, but he will have none of them, or almost none. This *synkoinonos* is an exception; it is a thoroughly Pauline word, being used at Rom 11:17; 1 Cor 9:23 and Phil 1:7, and it had no classical or earlier Scriptural use. Two other Pauline words of almost the same sense are used by John, *synergos* and *syndoulos*, the former in 3 Jn 8 and the latter in Apoc 6:11; 19:10 and 22:9. It may be that these three words had become so familiar that their use was unavoidable, while other words which still bore upon them the signs of their Pauline origin were avoided by John.

XVIII

Kosmos: the World

WHEN the brethren of the Lord (in 7:4) said to Him: "Show yourself to the world," what did they mean? They were thinking in the context of a journey to Jerusalem for the feast of Tabernacles, and to the Jewish mind Jerusalem was the centre of the world, even though there would not have been such a concourse of visitors there at that time as there was for Passover. If He sought to be in men's mouths for His deeds, that was where He ought to be. (*Codex Bezae* has seen the difficulty here by its change of "Judaea" into "Galilee" in verse 3; Galilee of the Gentiles may have been thought to give a better cross-section of the world.) They are quickly given their answer. "The world cannot find it within itself to hate you; it has not that disposition [for the sense of 'to be able' here, see Wisd 11:20]. You are too much inclined to accept its valuations. But Me it hates because I show it up."

Our Lord had to make a slight shift of emphasis in his antithesis of the world and His followers. To a Jew there was God's elect, and the heathen with their godlings, the vast *Goim*. The distinction of the two was based on circumcision and acceptance of the Law. That would pass away with the coming of Christianity but the revelation of that fact was to be held up till the reception of Cornelius (Ac 10) according to the disposition of Providence, and hence a vague term could serve in the meantime to conceal the gap in the plan. Baptism, with a renunciation of the world, would be

the basis of the distinction between followers of Christ and the world, and this would be the only basis for distinction. But the distinction would not mean the same as that between elect and reprobate, and so the old language about heathen *Goim* could not be retained.

That this change of emphasis was due to Christ Himself, and is not just a reading-back by John into gospel times of what came later, may be seen by comparing Mt 5:14 with Jn 9:5. While Christ is in the world, He is the Light of the world; and in the sermon on the Mount the disciples are told they are the Light of the world. The world is then in neither phrase wholly abandoned to iniquity, nor made a formal principle equal and opposite to the good. The sense of both sayings is the same, and no claim that John is innovating can stand without evidence. But, if the world is enlightened by Christ, or by His apostles, this light can be for a judgment as well as for a help to salvation; the metaphor is well-chosen and worthy of Our Lord Himself. The friendly use of light to the world is illustrated in 11:9–10: "If a man walk in the twelve hours of daylight, then he has the light of the world to help him and can come to no harm. If he walk at night, he will stumble, not having light in himself" (for in Jewish thought there had to be an inner source in the recipient of light, as well as the outer diffusion-source). In 3:19–20 the other use of light in the world is exemplified. Men have loved darkness rather than light (and so it shows them up and helps towards their judgment). They hate the light and will not face it because it is showing them up in their evil works. Here more than anywhere one finds the transitional sense of the term "the world". Not all is rooted in evil; there is a groping and sometimes a scurrying hither and thither. Some are committed to

evil, and they move further back into the dark, while others hover undecidedly or just cling together in a large inert mass. As the term "kingdom" for the Synoptics has the meaning of something that has begun its realization but is not yet installed in its perfection, this term "world" is a negative counterpart of "kingdom", and a realized eschatology may be applied to it. There *was* a time of darkness, but that is gradually being done away, so that in a true sense one can speak of it as past, but it is not fully past and gone for good.

Hence the need for overcoming the world, just as much as for advancing the kingdom. The phrase is used in 1 Jn 5:4–5 and is there linked with baptism, which is the primary act of overcoming, but not the end. In Apoc there is plenty said about "overcoming" but, strangely enough, it is never assigned an object; the verb is used by itself (2:7, 11, 17, 26 and 3:5, 12, 21). In each of the 7 letters to churches, "overcoming" is mentioned and never once its object. Even later in the book (5:5; 6:2; 21:7) the same lack is observed. Obviously the object to be supplied is "the world". That this did not need saying was due to the spread of the baptismal catechesis in which formal instruction about renunciation of the world had been given. In Apoc 2:26 we have a valuable extension of the phrase: "He who overcometh and keepeth until the end My works"; this indicates the transitional nature of "the world"; it is on the way out, but it will be there in some shape or form till the end.

That being so, what is the world's principle of cohesion? What keeps it in being, or prevents it going out like a spent wick? In 16:11 there is the Prince of the world introduced; he has been mentioned in 14:30 as having no claim on Christ, though no doubt wishing to

establish one. It is precisely his over-reaching himself that brings about his downfall, though one has not to bring in any "mousetrap-theory" of the Redemption to justify the idea. One has not to say that Christ baited a trap for the Devil and, when it was entered, set it off. Judas was not exactly a bait; the regrets for him in the prayer of 17:12 are enough to preclude that. It is rather the aggression of Satan that is to blame for his fall. The death of Christ, which is his judgment, is the proto-type of many victories over the world, for it is that which gives substance to the rite of baptism by which that victory is applied to the individual.

The early age of Christianity saw another and more immediate result of this judgment of Satan; the freeing of his captives. The vision of Apoc 20 shows us what John thought of Satan being himself bound and made captive, but he does not advert to the setting free of the captives in the harrowing of Hell. The fate of the patriarchs, which is mysteriously glimpsed at in 1 Pet, does not seem to figure at all in the Johannine theology. Abraham rejoiced to see that day of Christ, but we are not given any enlargement on the subject. The line of patriarchs that are in Heb 12 commended for their faith has a supporting line in 1 Clem 10–12 (Abraham, Lot, Rahab), and in 1 Clem 17 it is said: "Let us become imitators of those also who went about in goatskins and sheepskins preaching the coming of Christ, i.e. Elias, Eliseus, and Ezechiel too, the prophets, and besides them men of good report." To what, apart from this, do we owe the practice of the early Church of depicting far more frequently the men of the OT than those of the NT in all the material that has survived? Why should John stand aside from this line of thought? Perhaps it is part of his policy of limiting and keeping within due

bounds veneration for John the Baptist. A clue in this direction is the fact that when Clement of Alexandria quotes the extract just cited from 1 Clem 17 he adds quite spontaneously the name of the Baptist to the list of those who went about in goatskins. The last of the prophets may indeed have been the first to benefit from the victory over Satan gained by the death of Christ, but that was no reason why the evangelist would want to tarry over it himself.

Since the world is a transitional term, it cannot be hated by Christ in the way the God of the Manichees hated the *massa damnata* that was opposed to him. Some of it will yet be won over and hence the striking sayings in John about such mysteries as Christ giving His flesh "for the life of the world" (6:51) or (3:16) that God so loved the world . . . ; these are meant to be striking, though their repetition has made them seem like platitudes. Or perhaps people make up for themselves some kind of convention, that "world" in these contexts means something else from what it does in other parts of the gospel, and so blunt the sharpness of the sayings. There are limits. Jesus does not pray for "the world" (17:9), for that would be to desire its continuance, and for Christ that would be a contradiction. John has no qualms about telling us that Christ loved the world and that we ourselves must not (1 Jn 2:15), for he can expect us to understand. That he could do so himself may have been in part due to his vision (Apoc 11:15) of the opening of the seventh seal, when: "The kingdom of the world is become that of the Lord and of His Christ." The fact of having lived through the years following on the murder of Nero would have given John's imagination plenty of material about the transfer of empire on which the vision could draw. In even the smallest town

there would be the group of men chiselling away the name of the just-fallen emperor from the plaques and inscriptions in consequence of his *damnatio memoriae*; there would be the lapse of some feast-days and rituals and the initiation of others; new slogans for old on the coins, and perhaps a change of governor in the neighbourhood.

John's final word on the matter (1 Jn 5:19) is to say that the world "lieth wholly in the power of the evil One". From this some apologists of the second and third centuries would evolve the idea that Satan had been the angel entrusted with the government of all that concerned this earth, all that was sublunary. John does not go quite so far. Wheresoever in the world the gospel has not gone, there is the power of evil, but: "I have sent you that you should go forth and bear fruit . . ."

XIX

The Jews

O F the seventy times that the word occurs in the gospel of John some can be at once left aside as conventional labels. When Gentiles speak in the narrative of the gospel, they have to refer to "the Jews" with that title. Thus the Samaritan woman (4:9) utters the famous line: "Jews and Samaritans do not mix", a line omitted by *codex Bezae*, which is notably anti-Jewish. Similarly in 18:35, Pilate's astonished question: "Am I a Jew?" is to be taken in the most general sense. The footnotes that John provides for his reader about Jewish feasts and customs have similar labels. Thus in 2:6: "The manner of purification of the Jews", or 19:40: "The manner in which the Jews prepare for burial", and the many mentions of feasts (2:13; 5:1; 7:2; 11:55; 19:42) are presumably put there to help a Gentile reader at Ephesus or elsewhere. It would be hard to explain them if one took quite literally the idea of Professor van Unnik that John's gospel was written for a synagogue of the Jews of the Diaspora, probably in Asia Minor. It is true that there is much Messianic argument in the gospel, but the presence of these notes points to a wider audience; one could hardly speak to the Jews of Ephesus and tell them: "Now it was the feast of the Jews . . ."

The title "King of the Jews" John has in the Passion-story, just as it is found in the Synoptics (18:33 and 39; 19:3, 14, 19–21; cf. Mt 27:11, 29, 37 which are parallel). John has added the episode of the challenge to Pilate

about the title, and it may be here that he begins to suggest a difference of meaning in the term: "Write not, King of the Jews, but that he said: 'I am the King of the Jews.' " The official spokesmen of the Jews thus take the initiative in making a distinction between "Jews" and "What Jesus called Jews"; by a Johannine irony this distinction will be turned against themselves. Pilate (19:14) has proclaimed Jesus king of the Jews, and they have replied that they have no king but Caesar. It is in view of this rejection that the irony of John enters into the story. But can we think of John as reading back into the Passion-story a conclusion that he had come to in the light of his visions of Patmos? In Apoc 2:9 and 3:9 (the letters to Smyrna and Philadelphia) he speaks in identical terms of: "those who say they are Jews but are not, for they are the synagogue of Satan." These are said to afflict Smyrna with some kind of blasphemy, while Philadelphia is promised the homage of some of these, presumably through their conversion. Now it happens that we hear soon after John's time of the Jews of Smyrna who are active in the martyrdom of Polycarp (who must have been the "angel of the church at Smyrna" even in John's day). "The Jews were on the alert," say the Acts, "when we intended to take his body out of the fire . . . When the centurion saw the disturbance the Jews were making, he declared the body public property." (*Acts of Polycarp* 17, 18). But this hostility, for all that it may account for the strong language of Apoc 2:9, was not a new thing in the early second century; it had been on the go for a long time. One can find a trace of it in the Synoptics, in Mt 4:23; 9:35; 10:17; 12:9; 13:54 and above all 23:34. "Your synagogues", in this passage, implies that they are not "my synagogues"; hence the general

use in Mt of the term "*their* synagogues". If one had asked at the time: "Whose synagogues?" the answer would have had to be: "The Jews' " and we would be already in possession of the Johannine terminology where "the Jews" can be used in a hostile sense for "those who hated Jesus", cf. 5:16; 6:41; 7:1; 8:22–23; 10:31 etc. It is quite unhistorical to say that the Synoptics wrote "when they were aware that Jewish leaders and public opinion in Palestine opposed the preaching of the gospel, but they did not foresee how the schism in the Jewish people was going to end, whereas John, when he wrote, knew how it had ended and imported into his gospel something from this result". Justin (*dial Tryph.* 17:1; and 108:2–3) tells how, when the Jews saw the resurrection and ascension, not only did they refuse to believe, but: "choosing out envoys from Jerusalem, you sent them into the whole world, saying that an atheist heresy of Christians has arisen, and compiling a list of charges from what those who are ignorant of our belief say about us." In the second passage he gives a more carefully dated account: "When you learnt about His resurrection . . ., you sent into the whole world, as I said before, envoys whom you had chosen, to declare that a wicked and atheist heresy had arisen, coming from a certain Jesus of Galilee, a seducer whom we crucified. . . . What is more, when your city was captured and its site laid waste, you did not repent but had the effrontery to curse Him and all who believed in Him." This allusion to the addition to the 18 Benedictions of an anathema against the Minim is historically correct, for the addition was made soon after 70. It does not seem unreasonable then to take the other part of Justin's statement as correct in time, and that places the sending

of Jewish "Apostles" to circulate charges against the
Christians well before the First Revolt. If that is so, one
cannot maintain that the Synoptic writers were not yet
aware how the schism was going to end, whereas John
was. The real divide comes at the latest with the arrest
of Paul in the temple (about the year 57). After that,
there could be no hope; that was the whole point of his
appeal to Caesar. It is perhaps significant that the later
calumnies against the Christians for alleged canni-
balism, incest and onolatry are used by pagans against
the Jews themselves at a somewhat earlier time. The
history of the Samaritan Thallus may also have helped
in the same direction, for the one fragment that has
survived of his work tells of an attempt to explain away
the darkness at the crucifixion as being due to an
eclipse. Such an explanation could well have been part
of the general answer to the Christian preaching.

John for his part is aware that the rejection of Christ
by the Jews was not complete and monolithic. In 7:31;
8:31; 10:42; 11:45; 12:11 he stresses that many Jews
believed in Jesus. This belief was in some cases transi-
tory, for the episode of 8:31–33 ends with an attempted
stoning. The Lazarus episode is especially instructive
about the two-way split in the Jewish attitude, for there
(11:45–46) it comes to a head; many believed, but some
went to the Pharisees and they had the Sanhedrin meet
to plot against Him.

It cannot be said that John has slanted the Passion-
story against the Jews. He is the first to make clear that
Roman soldiers (the cohort with its *tribunus militum*,
18:3 and 18:12) take part with the ὑπηρέται from the
temple in the arrest in Gethsemani. Nor can one claim
that John (19:16–17) has put the crucifixion in the
hands of the Jews rather than of the Romans, for he is

quite clear that, "the soldiers indeed did these things", and in his work, as in the Synoptics, soldiers = Romans. He is only repeating the Synoptics when he says: "Then Pilate gave Him to them that he might be crucified" (cf. Mt 27:26). It is true that John adds: "And they took Him,"[1] but immediately he continues: "and carrying His own cross He went out . . ." The emphasis on the trial before Pilate and the lack of interest in what happened before the high priest may be due to his desire to present (18:31–32) the changed course of the trial as a fulfilment of the prophecies of crucifixion. If the Jews had gone ahead with the trial themselves, they would have stoned Him, but as they had to fall back on the Romans, it turned into a crucifixion.

It cannot be said that John is unhistorical in making the Jews say they have no right of life and death. It is true that they had it for the safeguarding of the temple area, according to the terms of the inscription that was set up there. But this is a concession that Rome was quite willing to make to local religious feeling. The cases cited which are supposed to show that they did have power to kill are of no value as proof. The affair of Stephen is a piece of lynch-law and can be most probably dated to the *interregnum* when Pilate had gone away and the new man had not yet arrived to succeed him. The death of James in 62 is a clear case of the same thing, and we are told by Josephus that the new governor deposed the high priest when he found out what had happened during the *interregnum*. The only other instance is that of the burning of the daughter of a priest taken in sin; this incident cannot be dated, but it is quite feasible that it happened in the reign of MJ Agrippa I (37–45) when Roman control was entirely

[1] The *eduxerunt* of Vg is not in the Greek text.

withdrawn from Judaea and it was for the king and the high priest to run the country.

The curious affair of 3:25, a dispute of the disciples of John with "Jews" about purification, might be a point of impact of Qumran on the story of Jesus. The location was not far from Qumran and the topic was one that must have been much canvassed there. "No one is to go into water to attain the purity of holy men. For men cannot be purified except they repent their evil" (*Manual*, p. 57). "No novice is to be admitted to the purity of the whole community until after a full year his spiritual outlook and his conduct have been examined" (*ibid.* p. 60). "A man who deliberately lies about his wealth is to be regarded as outside the purity entailed by membership" (*ibid.* p. 61). The other side in the dispute of 3:25 were just "Jews", not yet "the Jews".

The full sense of "the Jews" in John is that of typology. In the OT there are plenty of places where the faithlessness of God's people is castigated. John uses some of these (e.g. Ps 68:4 in 15:25) on his own, but the theme of rejection is already stamped on the gospel of Matthew. John was no pioneer in this. The whole pattern of the gospel of Matthew seems to be that of a twofold rejection, that of the Baptist in its first half (where Christ is presented as coming in the place of the Baptist) and that of Christ Himself in the second half (where the Church is presented as coming in the place of Christ). John does not show concern about the rejection of the Baptist, perhaps for reasons already alluded to, but he is certainly alive to the second theme of Matthew, just as he is to Matthew's presentation of Christ as the Second Moses.

XX

Living Water

ON the seven days of the feast of Tabernacles there was a procession in which a golden flagon of water was carried from the Pool of Siloe and was poured out as libations in the temple in memory of the water that Moses drew from the rock. Isaias 12:3 was sung on this occasion: "Ye shall draw waters with joy from the fountains of salvation, and shall say in that day: 'Give praise to Jahwe; call upon His name; declare among the nations His deeds, put them in mind that His name has been exalted'." The rabbinical enlargement of the story by the miracle of the rock following the Israelites through the desert was obviously current in Our Lord's time, if Paul (1 Cor 10:3) was able to allude to it without more ado in a passing phrase. His "taking over" of this story, by the declaration that "the rock was Christ", shows that he had already come across something of what John has put into 7:37–38.

There has been some discussion whether Jesus spoke on the seventh day of the feast, while the procession would still be going on, or on the eighth, when there was no procession, but when there was the equivalent of a Sabbath rest and special sacrifices were held (TB *Sukkah* 5). In either case the intention to "take over" the Jewish rite, to claim to give it much deeper meaning when it is transferred to Christ, is plain enough. "As water giveth life to the world, so do the words of the Torah give life to the world", said the Rabbis, and this function of life-giving law Jesus had already taken to

Himself in the sermon on the Mount with His refrain: "I say unto you." "The origin of truth lies in the fountain of light", says the *Manual of Discipline*. "Like waters of purification God will sprinkle upon man the spirit of truth to cleanse him of all the abominations of falsehood and of all pollution through the spirit of uncleanness, to the end that being made upright men may have transcendental knowledge and the lore of the sons of heaven" (p. 55). The equating of water from heaven with knowledge is quite characteristic of Jewish Gnosticism and reappears when Origen comes to interpret this text of John. How far Origen was original in his importation of material from Philo to help to explain the text is not clear, but he probably had some (Jewish-Christian) forerunners. He is the first who vouches for the reading of the text which is current in most versions of today. This requires a stop after the words, "let him come to me and let him drink." Then what follows refers to the individual Christian and not to Christ Himself. "As the Scripture says: 'He that believeth in Me, out of his belly shall flow streams of living water'."

Origen, seeing in the Jewish idea of water above the firmament a clue to the passage, says boldly: "Let each of you strive to become a distributor of that water that is above (and below), so that streams of living water, that is the understanding that is heavenly water and the sharing of that which comes from above, may be caused to flow from the belly of each and rise up into life eternal" (*hom. in Gen* 1:2; GCS 29:3). The Christian is the distributor of the heavenly revealed doctrine. When he comes to the episode (Gen 26:18) of Isaac digging wells ("They digged in the torrent and found living water"), Origen says: "Since our Isaac is come amongst us, let us receive Him and dig our wells; let us take the

earth from them and cleanse them from all filth and from all muddied and earthly thoughts, and we shall find in them living water, about which the Lord said: 'He who believeth in Me, from his belly shall flow living waters' " (*hom. in Gen* 13:3; GCS 29:118). It is to be noted that Origen assumes that the well is in the mind or heart of each Christian; thoughts are to be purified, and then the revelation flows abundantly. In particular the understanding of the spiritual sense of Holy Scripture is taken to be this living water. The true Christian will (*hom. in Num* 12:2; GCS 30:100) bring out spiritual understanding of Scripture from the inner rock where Christ is. In *hom in Exod* 11:2, GCS 29:254) he even takes Jn 19:34 in this way: "This rock, if it had not been struck, would not give forth its waters; but being pierced has given us the waters of the NT . . . For if He had not been pierced, so that there came out of His side blood and water, we should all have suffered from a thirst for the word of God."

What then is Origen's OT parallel which he would suppose to be alluded to here? The answer seems to be Prov 5:15–16: "Drink water out of thy own cistern and the streams of thy own well. Let NOT thy fountains overflow, but in thy own streets let thy waters be distributed." (The LXX insert a negative in the second part of this passage, and Origen noted this. So *hom. in Num* 12:1; GCS 30:94.) For the Jew of the second century the text was already a capital one; Aqiba had said of it that it showed how a Rabbi was a source of living water; from him came disciples and the disciples of them; while Rabbi Meir (*Pirke Aboth* 6:1) had said that one who understands the Torah is a fountain of water for others.

Ambrose (who followed Origen and Basil mostly in

his exegesis) carries the idea a little further when he says that the fountain is the Holy Spirit: "This stream flowing from the throne of God (Apoc 22:1) is the Holy Spirit who is imbibed by those who believe in Christ, according to the words: 'If any man thirst, let him come . . .' " (*de Spir. sco* 3:20; PL 16:812). The closing words of Jn 7:39 are a justification for this correction by Ambrose, but Origen might have said that, in talking about the spiritual sense of Scripture, he was particularizing upon one of the works of the Holy Spirit and not considering the whole range of His activity. 1 Jn 5:10, according to a widely supported reading, says that he who believeth in the Son of God hath the witnessing *in himself*, and this witnessing is the work of the Spirit, as well as that of water and blood. The reading is in *Sinaiticus* and the Vulgate, while *Alexandrinus* has an addition that makes for the same result; these Egyptian Greek MSS. are perhaps held to the interpretation that Origen would have favoured, while more independent scribes kept the more difficult reading: "Hath the testimony in Him," i.e. in the Spirit, or in Christ who is the chief witness or martyr. But it is time now to see how widespread is the support of the alternative reading of Jn 7:37–38.

Irenaeus (*adv. haer.* 5:18:2 H) has no doubt: "The Spirit is in all of us, and He is the living water that the Lord gives to those who have a right belief in Him." He must have read (with *codex Bezae* etc.): "If a man thirst, let him come; and let him drink who believeth in me. As the Scripture saith: 'Out of his belly shall flow rivers of living water'." There is also the famous passage (*ibid.* 3:24:1 H): "Where there is the Church, there is the Spirit of God, and where the Spirit of God, there the Church and all grace. Now the Spirit is truth.

Wherefore those who do not partake of Him are not nourished by the breasts of their mother, nor do they drink of the clear stream that comes from the side of Christ." The Bodmer papyrus (P 66) which may be as old as Irenaeus, has a stop after "let him drink", but it is only fair to say that the placing of stops by this scribe was a very erratic business. On the preceding page he put one stop at the end of a sentence and one in the middle of another, and that was all the punctuation he deigned to give for some six verses, while on the page where this text is found he has a stop between two parts of one word, another where a question ends, and the third in the place already mentioned. Thus the papyrus has no real light to throw on the problem of this reading, except to show how easy it might be for an alteration of phrasing to arise.

Justin had this reading before Irenaeus, and seems to have taken the more realistic understanding of the text before the Gnosis of Origen had transformed it. He says: (dial. 114.1): "We rejoice to die for the sake of the name of the Rock that is so fair and that wells up with living water for the hearts of those who, through Him, love the Father of all, and that provides drink for those who wish to drink the water of life." But what Scripture passage do the partisans of this reading envisage as being appealed to? Cyprian is in favour of Isai 43:18–21: " 'If they thirst in the desert,' saith Isaias, 'He will bring them water; from the rock will He bring it for them; the rock shall be cloven, and water shall flow and my people shall drink.' And this is fulfilled in the gospel when Christ, who is the rock, is pierced by the blow of the lance in His passion. He warns us what had been foretold by the prophet when He proclaims: 'If any man thirst let him come, and let him drink who

believeth in Me.' As the Scripture saith: 'Streams of living water shall flow from His belly'." (*ep.* 63:8; CSEL 3:706).

Another OT episode was read into the text by the so-called *Tractatus Origenis* (ascribed to Gregory of Elvira); when Moses threw wood from a certain tree into the bitter waters to make them sweet (Exod 15:25), he was foreshadowing the cross, "which makes the waters of baptism sweet, so that they can satisfy those who thirst, and hence the Lord said, as He stood in the Temple: 'Let him who thirsts come and let him drink strength from water without charge'." Melito in his homily on the Pasch (85) speaks in the style of the *Improperia*: "This is He that gave thee manna in the desert, that gave thee to drink from the rock, that gave thee laws on Horeb, that gave thee a portion in the promised land. . . ."

Sometimes the Fathers draw into the picture the other "living water" passages of John (e.g. 6:35), whilst the earliest paintings that have to do with baptism show Moses striking the rock alongside the Samaritan woman with her pitcher at the well. On the façade of the cathedral of Monza there is a relief in the lunette over the West door where Christ is depicted standing naked, but superimposed on His body is a pyramidal structure reaching as far as the navel from the ground and carved to represent water. This would seem to be a Lombardic attempt to illustrate the text of John, rather than a simple depicting of the baptism in the Jordan.

XXI

The Sign of the Woman

THE earliest commentary on Apoc 12 is that of Victorinus of Pettau. He wrote about 300 A.D. and had the use of the work of Papias; his work therefore puts us in touch with the Johannine circle at Ephesus, for it is on record that Papias strongly championed the inspired character of Apoc when opposition to its acceptance was being fostered in the second century. Papias was himself from Asia Minor and had some kind of link with the Johannine school. The work of Victorinus has not long been known in its original form, for it was pirated and adapted by Jerome. Only in 1916 was the true text of Victorinus made available, though much of what he had written had been for long accepted as the work of Jerome. On Apoc 12:1–3 he has this to say: "The woman is the ancient Church of patriarchs and prophets and of the holy apostles, because she had the groans and torture of her longing until such time as there came out of her own people and her own flesh the Promise, made in olden time." The mantle of the sun is "the hope of resurrection and the promise of glory"; the moon is, "the fate of the bodies of the saints who have died", while the crown of twelve stars, "signifies that of the Fathers according to fleshly birth, for from them was the Divinity destined to take flesh." [1] Traditionally there were twelve patriarchs, and the apocryphal *Testament of the Twelve Patriarchs* canonized this idea.

[1] *Patrum significat secundum carnis nativitatem, ex quibus erat Spiritus carnem sumpturus.*

131

On the dragon Victorinus has this comment: "He who was not born of the seed of man owed nothing to death, and on that account the dragon could not devour Him." By an easy transfer Victorinus has passed from the female Church and her longings for a Redeemer to Our Lady and her Child. Once one can look upon the Church as existing from the time of Abel, the analogy is clear and the transfer does not appear violent. Now it can be shown that this way of regarding the Church was traditional long before Victorinus; it is in the work of Hermas. In his story of his visions (8:1) he tells how after there had appeared to him an elderly lady clad in shining garments who carried a book in her hands, on another day he saw a young man of great beauty. He was asked by this young man who the lady was who had shown him her book. " 'The Sibyl', said I. 'You're wrong; she's not.' 'Who, then, is she?' said I. 'She is the Church,' he said. 'Why then is she old,' I asked. 'Because she was created before everyone else; that's why she's old, and for her sake the world was brought into being.' " If the patriarchs were saved by their faith in a Redeemer to come, they could be said to belong to the Church in some sense, though not baptized. Melito in his homily on the Pasch asks: "Do you wish to see the mystery of the Lord? Look on Abel that was slain like Him, on Isaac that was tethered like Him, on Joseph that was sold like Him, on Moses that was exposed like Him, on David that was pursued like Him, on the prophets that suffered in like manner with Christ." Of Abel himself the liturgy says (in the *Preface* for the consecration of an altar): "Abel, the forerunner in his passion of the mystery of salvation." A case could be made out for the Jewish origin of this idea of the pre-existing Church, for the Rabbis seem to have

believed that God created the world for the sake of Moses and of the Chosen People. When the Church began to claim that she was the true Israel—and this was not delayed till the second century—it would be quite consonant for her to accept also this idea of pre-existence. The eloquent passage in Hebr 11 about the faith that saved the patriarchs would provide a justification for the take-over, if that were needed.

The reason for the slowness of the change in patristic times from the idea that the Church is the woman clothed with the sun to that of the Blessed Virgin may be found in what is said about the pain of travail. There was a tradition of the painless birth of Christ which can be traced back to the end of the first century, where it is found in the *Odes of Solomon*. In the course of time this tradition was much elaborated, providing a basis for the Apocryphal Gospels to build upon, as they do so readily with stories about the midwives at Bethlehem, even before the end of the second century. Now with the emphasis of Apoc 12:2 on the pains ("She cries out with the birth-pains and is under torture until she give birth") it would seem quite wrong to ascribe this to Our Lady, whereas for the Church there would not be the same difficulty. Had not St. Paul said that he was "in travail once again for you Galatians, till Christ be formed in you" (Gal 4:19).

Tichonius, the Donatist and contemporary of Augustine, in his commentary on Apoc 12 wrote: "In the woman he has designated the Church, who has at baptism clothed herself with Christ the sun of justice. The moon is the heretical church, the stars the twelve apostles. Ever with torment does the Church give birth to Christ. She suffers torment in her birth-pains, either until the multitude of Gentiles has been gathered

together, or until the false dissemblers are ejected from her womb." Finally he adds: "The Church gave birth to Christ who, though He was God, did not disdain to be born a man." One can see that for him Our Lady is the antitype of the Church, and that this is so obvious as not to call for an explanation.

The earliest author whom Fr. H. Rahner can cite in his book on *Our Lady and the Church*, when he is enumerating those who refer the text primarily to Our Lady, is "the pseudo-Augustine", i.e. a sermon that has been wrongly ascribed to Augustine. Alcuin and Haymo of Halberstadt are the chief possibilities; they belong to the ninth century, and it would be difficult to date this pseudo-Augustine very much earlier. Oecumenios, a sixth century Greek, has also been cited. What we can see in the sixth century is that the two figures are practically equivalent. The hymn to the Church in the *Bangor Antiphonary* from this time is a valuable witness:

Christo regina apta	Virgo valde fecunda
Solis luce amicta	Haec, et mater intacta.
Simplex, simulque docta	Laeta et tremebunda,
Undecunque invicta.	Verbo Dei subacta.

Parallel to this Irish text there is the prayer in the Armenian rite for consecrating a church where what seems to be a litany of Our Lady turns out to be a hymn of praise of the Church. This Armenian prayer is not much later than the Bangor hymn. When the adapters had to assign to Our Lady the pains that are described in the text they never refer to her childbirth, but (e.g. with Hugh of St. Cher) to the pain of her innermost heart, "when she came to her martyrdom at the passion of her Son", or perhaps to the birth from her of the mystical Body of Christ, though this latter idea cannot

be documented before Cornelius a Lapide, and it is in any case transferred to Our Lady from the female figure of the Church.

Fr. Gächter has pointed out (*Maria im Erdenleben*, p. 220) how the only two passages in the gospel where John introduces Our Lady form an *inclusio* after the Jewish manner; she is addressed as Woman at the beginning of the gospel when the first miracle is done at Cana and again she is addressed by the same title when the work of Redemption is about to be consummated. In the first the *kairos* is not come, in the second it is. This *kairos* is Messianic, and one may therefore regard the title of Woman as Messianic, reaching back to the promise of Gen 3:15. The fulfilling of the Scripture seems to have been very much the preoccupation of John in his crucifixion-narrative; he adverts to it in verses 24, 28, 30, 36, 37 of chapter 19. John's normal word is "carry out" the Scripture, so in 12:38; 13:18; 15:25; 17:12; and even here at 19:24 and 36, but for the vital passage 19:28 he has changed to "complete". Some of the scribes, especially *Sinaiticus*, *Bezae* and the Old Latin have kept πληρωθῇ here, but the less usual word must be right; it means that all the Messianic signs had been given to the Jews in full. But what sort of a Messianic sign was the commending of His mother to John and of John to His mother? If we regard the word "woman" as a clue, it might be claimed that the enmity between the serpent and the woman of Gn 3:15–19 is involved. The seed of the woman has crushed the serpent's head, but that work is to go on. The recurrence of the figure in Apoc 12:3, where the dragon pursues the woman and the woman is the Church, assures us of that. Hence there has to be a pledge of continuity. One of the apostles is there, and

he will do. Jesus has often spoken of their office to carry on His work; here it is put in the context of the first and last Messianic prophecy. One may admit that the "taking unto his own" by John is not quite fitted into this picture. The words "unto his own" are used 1:11 and 16:32; they seem to have a local sense in both cases. Why should John bother us with that detail now, in the height of events? It may be one of his indications of vital testimony; he is hinting that he knows what he is talking about, because it was to his abode that Our Lady went. Some have thought that there is a polemic against the "brethren of the Lord" intended; it was not *their* business now to interfere. Hoskyns is more probably right in seeing a contrast with 16:32 and the "other disciples" who fled each to his own place.

It is worth noting with Hoskyns (p. 509) that John is the only one who uses the word "garden" for Gethsemani and who tells us that the tomb was in a garden. It may be that he wants to recall Genesis once more (God walking in the garden, just as the gardener walks there, to be met by Magdalen) for Christ undid the work of Adam in the garden.

XXII

The Image of the Beast

DANIEL in his visions saw four beasts come out
of the sea, one a winged lioness, one a bear, one
a winged leopard and finally a beast with
many horns and with teeth of iron. In Jewish popular
tradition by the time of Our Lord this last beast was
understood to be Rome with her formidable array of
legionaries armed with the *pilum*. The relevance of this
vision of Daniel (7:1–14) for John was that it immediately preceded the vision of the Son of Man on the
clouds of heaven. John (18, 24 and 28) has nothing to
report about what Our Lord said to Caiaphas, though
he must have known the account in the Synoptics in
which the prophecy of Daniel is quoted.

In the interval between the ascension and the time
of writing of the gospel, John has come to see a little
further into the mystery of the beast. Apoc 6:8 tells of
the coming of the pale horse and after him the putting
of men to death by sword, starvation and by the beasts
of the earth. These were the penalties levied on those
who refuse emperor-worship when challenged about it.
It is true that Trajan, in his famous reply to Pliny, wrote
conquirendi non sunt (they are not to be hunted down) and
that anonymous denunciations were to be set aside, but,
whatever the law which they were thought to be trans-
gressing by being Christians, it was not easy, especially
at moments of crisis or popular anxiety, for Christians
to escape all questioning. If they stood firm, then they
might look forward to "indignities and tortures",

"women being persecuted as Danaids and in the guise
of Dirce, suffering terrible and impious indignities, but
completing the race of faith," as Clement (*ep.* 6:2) has
told us. The Danaids in Greek myth had to fill a cask
with water, while seeing it run out through holes at the
bottom; Dirce was tied to the horns of a bull and so
dragged to death; the contemporary popular taste for
mimes (dumb-show performance of the legends, with
no dialogue but with occasional songs) could not be
satisfied by the professional performers (*mimi et mimae*)
where the story to be represented involved loss of life;
hence the idea that those condemned to death could be
made to take the part of victims, where the real actors
would be wild beasts. All this had happened before
John came to write his gospel, as the passage from
Clement assures us. It is therefore important to examine
whether John had allowed this harsh reality to colour
his recollection of the past when he came to write. Such
punishments had been in use for Christians since the
year 64; Tacitus speaks (*Annals* 15:44) of Christians
being in Nero's persecution exposed to outrage *ut fer-
arum tergis contecti laniatu canum interirent*, and thus the
significance of beast-imagery in John's apocalyptic
visions would be at once clear to him.

The vision of Apoc 13 combines elements from Daniel
with the new factors just mentioned. The beast (13:2)
was like Daniel's leopard, but had the feet of a bear
and the mouth of a lion, while there were many horns
on its head. It is not profitable to tarry over speculations
about the possible clues to the date of the vision supplied
by equating these horns with the line of Roman
emperors. Historians are wont to start with Augustus
but in the East there was a cult of Julius Caesar, and
even of Antony before that, and the rival emperors of

the years 68–70 make it very difficult to reach certainty in one's counting. The beast, be it noted, is a tetramorph, and thus a parody of the true tetramorph of the evangelists. This beast is the servant of the dragon, which in the preceding vision was seen to menace the Church and her offspring.

The grievous wound that the beast suffers, but from it recovers, (13:3) may signify the transfer from one *domus divina* to another, from the Julio-Claudians to the Flavians, who had to start up an emperor-worship for themselves from nothing, since they had not dynastic marriage-alliances to fall back upon. Alternatively, it may refer to Domitian's efforts to overcome some check to the growth of the cult of the Flavians.

John must have been convinced by this vision that the empire was an ally of Satan, according to what he says (13:4–5). "Power was given to it to do as it would, [see Dan 11:36] for a time and times and half a time" (for that is the meaning of the forty-two months). John here uses a studied ambiguity which was familiar to Jews, for whom sevens and fourteens and even half-sevens were an indication of vagueness about an exact date. (Cf. how Paul was uncertain about the date of his vision *ante annos quatuordecim* (2 Cor 12:2) and how he went up to Jerusalem after 14 years (Gal 2:1).) In Alexandria there were men who worshipped a serpent as the Good Spirit (*Agathos Daimon*) and according to a papyrus (*Pap. Oxyrhyn.* VII: 1021) Nero was given just this title of *Agathos Daimon* there. Later on, about 90–91, coins were struck in Alexandria showing a serpent riding on the back of a horse, just as Domitian had erected a large equestrian statue of himself in Rome. The beast and his master would be familiar images, not only to John on Patmos, but also to his readers at Ephesus or Alexandria.

The interjection of 13:9–10 by John (this is not part of his vision) is meant to temper the indignation that his account of the Satanic character of Roman rule may be expected to arouse in his readers. Are they to revolt? (They did not in 132, when the Jews revolted.) If a man is being taken off to prison, to prison he must go. If he were to take up the sword of resistance, he would be made to perish by the same. That is the meaning of "patience and the faith of the saints". It is not a doctrine of harmony between Church and State but it does not differ fundamentally from what had been laid down by Paul and the Synoptics. Paul had said that the civil power beareth not the sword in vain, and John is saying that though the Christians do not like the régime, they will find resistance no solution. Clement at the close of his epistle puts up a prayer for the emperor (who must have been at that time Domitian) in these terms: "May we have peace . . . as we are become obedient to Thy all-majestic and all-virtuous Name, and to our governors and rulers upon this earth. Thou, Lord, hast given them the authority of the kingdom by Thy magnificent and unutterable strength, that we might recognize the glory and honour Thou hast given them and might be subject to them, while in no way going against Thy will. Grant them, Lord, health, peace, concord and steadfastness, that they may wield the rulership Thou hast given them without offence . . ." John is not in essential disagreement with this. He would no doubt emphasize the clauses about "not going in any way against Thy will" and "wielding the rulership without offence". In 19:11 John had given faithfully Christ's teaching on the origin of civil power, and it is significant that Apoc 13:9–10 does not go back on this, even though it leaves much unsaid that would have to

be elaborated later, e.g. about the right of rebellion or the duty of the Christian community to take care of those (slaves) who fled to its protection when they were being forced by a pagan master to blaspheme.

The Jews had been exempt from the rigours of emperor-worship, and Tacitus, who had governed the province of Asia about 114, could put into the mouth of Titus the declaration that Christianity was a branch from the root of Judaism.[1] It may be that until the time of Hadrian (when the laws against the Jews were tightened) Christians had been able to derive some protection from this confusion. Pliny does not make this one of his queries to Trajan but he may have been influenced by it or felt that it obscured his judgment. Hadrian in his rescript to Fundanus laid it down that: "If our subjects of the provinces are able to support by evidence their *supplex libellus* against the Christians, let them take this course, but they must not fall to beseeching and mere clamour." The danger that Christians would lapse under pressure (whether social or financial, as well as that of threats) must have been ever present to John. He could not afford to let them become complacent. The warning against idolatry which closes his first epistle (1 Jn 5:21) is in effect John's last word to posterity, and it was needed.

The problems of the second beast are perhaps insoluble at present. It is introduced (Apoc 13:11) as a counterpart to the Lamb and is given the voice of Satan the dragon. It promotes adoration of the first beast who has recovered from the almost fatal dagger-thrust. It can work pseudo-miracles, even bringing fire from heaven (13:12–15), to promote the cult of the first

---

[1] Tacitus had probably not read Rom 11:17. His idea was that, if the root of Jewry was destroyed, the branch would wither.

beast. It gives its own mark, without which no one may buy or sell (13:16–17). Is this meant to illustrate the way the Flavians had to take up the emperor-worship from where the Julio-Claudians had left it, when the killing of Nero nearly brought the whole sordid cult to an end? Or does it tell us in veiled terms of the care Domitian was taking to promote the divinity of his deceased brother Titus, to whom he certainly decreed the title of *Divus* Titus? Or perhaps that the Asiarchs (and other *concilia* in other provinces, charged with care of the emperor-worship) have it in their power to make a man's life as a trader impossible if he will not take part with them? Such indirect pressure was not unknown in antiquity, any more than today, when a man may be invited time after time to "come on the square" if he wants to succeed in business.

The end of the beast is told later (Apoc 19:19–20). The army of the Logos is drawn up for battle while the beast and the kings of the earth and their legions face Him. The beast is taken prisoner and with him the false prophet who did bogus miracles before him and tricked men into taking the mark of the beast on them. This may glance at Simon Magus, who seems to have been in some ways the Father of the Gnostics.

XXIII

The Sending of the Apostles

IN the gospel of Mark the word "send" is used just once: "He sent them into the swine" (Mk 5:12). This is in extreme contrast with the usage of John who has some thirty times the recurring phrase: "he that sent me" or the like. The deputation that comes to John the Baptist ask for an explanation which they may take back "to those that sent us". John himself is found (1:33) speaking of "he that sent me to baptize" and then Christ Himself begins (4:34) to tell us about His doing the will of "Him that sent Me." From then on until the end of ch. 12 the phrase is found 18 times and always spoken by Christ, in reference to His Father. Once only in this part of the gospel (7:18) does Christ generalize: "He that speaks for himself seeks his own glory; but he that seeks the glory of him that sent him, he is true and there is no iniquity in him." An innovator is proud of his own originality, but the Son speaks for the Father, "for Him hath the Father sealed" (6:27). The relationship of sender and sent is not just the appointing of a messenger; there is the fact of a guarantee, an empowerment to act as plenipotentiary. In 3:33 the evangelist himself, reflecting on the episodes of the Baptist and of Nicodemus, says "he that takes the witness (of the one who comes from above) sets his seal thereto that God is true". John has this word for "sealing" in these two places of the gospel and nowhere else, save for some two parallel usages in Apoc (10:4; and 22:10), the latter which is based on Dan 8:26 and 12:4.

This sealing, when done by God, is much more than anything man can do. Theologically speaking, one might say that the act of faith, by which we give our attestation to God's revelation, bears a remote analogy to God's own attestation. The Spirit beareth witness to our spirit that we are the sons of God.

In the later part of the gospel, from 13 onwards, there is a development of the thought involved in this phrase about sending. First of all, there is another generalization in 13:16: "A-man-sent is not greater than he who sends him." The word *apostolos* is found here, for the only time in John, and it is not a technical term for apostle, since John never uses it as such, but simply stands for a verbal noun: "the-man-sent".[1] This passage is viewed as important, since Christ recalls it again at 15:20. It is based on Synoptic tradition, for there is a straightforward reminiscence of Mt 10:24. (John does not use the truncated version of the saying as found in Lk 6:40.) Matthew has the pair, slave–lord, but for the second pair has put disciple and master. John keeps slave–lord and for the second pair gives what he thinks are equivalents of disciple and master, i.e. man-sent and his sender. It is not clear what is meant by "doing these things" in the next verse (13:17). It may look back to the feet-washing, but then 13:16 has to be treated as a parenthesis and in view of its importance for the whole gospel this is unlikely to be right. More probably the meaning is "act upon this saying" (as "doing the truth" elsewhere in John means acting on it). It is the disciples who are being addressed and the affair of Judas is commented on in verse 18; it seems,

[1] Clement of Alexandria (fragment 22) cites an exactly similar use of *apostolos* from one whom he styles The Presbyter. Further examples may be seen in the *Lexicon of Patristic Greek*, s.v.

then, that the disciples are being asked to realize that they are "men-sent". The great mission of the Son from His Father has to have a counterpart in the mission of the apostles by the Son.

In 20:21 the formal sending of the apostles takes place; parallelism, not contrast between the two missions, is implied (as Barrett notes): "In the words, works and person of Jesus, men were veritably confronted by God Himself. It follows that in the apostolic mission of the Church the world is confronted not merely by a human institution but by Jesus the Son of God." One is glad to have this sincere avowal from a great Methodist commentator on John. Barrett goes on to say that as Jesus in His ministry was entirely dependent upon and obedient to the Father, who sealed and sanctified Him, and as Jesus acted in the power of the Spirit who rested upon Him, so the Church is the apostolic church only in virtue of the fact that Jesus sanctified it and breathed the Spirit into it. As Catholics we should go on from this to argue that the parallelism warrants us in our idea of the infallibility of the Church and the perennial status of apostles within it. Not merely for their own lifetime were the apostles set up in power, but until the end.

It might be thought that, with all John's emphasis on this phrase about "he that sent Me", he was innovating on the Synoptic tradition, but there is another verb, the one which gives us the noun "apostle", which is frequently used in the Synoptics by Christ in just the same way and which does appear in John, though less frequently. Mt 10:40; 15:24; 21:37; have parallels in the other Synoptics. John 3:17; 3:34; 5:36; 6:29; 6:57; 7:29; 8:42; 10:36; 11:42; and then frequently in the sacerdotal prayer (17:3–25) are sufficient proof that

John has not discarded the term beloved of the Synoptics, but regards it as a synonym for the other word *pempein*, which he uses habitually. One apparent discrepancy in 17:18 may be noted. Here Jesus makes the sending (analogous to His own) that He will repeat in 20:21. He uses the past tense here and cannot therefore be looking ahead to what is to come after the Resurrection. Barrett's comment on this does not quite clear up the puzzle. "The aorist is used of the sending of the disciples although they are in fact not sent until 20:21. John writes from the standpoint of his own age, but also regards the mission of the Son as virtually completed . . . at the Last Supper . . ." There is such a thing as a timeless aorist, and that is what is wanted here to indicate the perennial character of the sending of the apostles; once it is begun, it goes on; they are given a status and not just a commission which will lapse with their death. One can see how abiding was this characteristic of "being sent" which John saw in Christ from the play he makes with the name of the pool of Siloe (9:7). The blind man has to go to "the-sent-one", just as the unbelieving one must come to Christ. From this pool was drawn the water for the procession to the temple during the feast of Tabernacles about which so much is said in 7:30–39. It is not surprising really that so many things in John should combine in this way; he had had abundant opportunity to allow the less relevant features to drop out and wither away in the course of a long lifetime of meditation on what he had been taught.

The sending of the Spirit is twice spoken of (14:26 and 15-26); the Father will send Him in the name of Jesus and Jesus will send Him from the Father. The fulfilment of this promise comes in 20:21, so that it is made

obvious that the Spirit is upon the Church through the apostles. In later theology the mission of the Spirit will be distinguished from the proceeding, the latter being reserved to the inner life of the godhead, the former seen in the midst of creation, and notably in the Church, where there is a visible mission of the Spirit at Pentecost and an invisible one at such times as the Church acts for Christ with supreme authority (e.g. in the decrees of a general council) and also at every Mass, where the priest is entrusted to act in the person of and with the power of Christ and by using His words sends the Spirit upon the bread and wine.

The short passage in 1 Jn 4:9–14 sums up his theology of sending. God's charity is disclosed by His sending His only-begotten Son to be the life of the world and ours in particular; and this He does by becoming a sin-offering for us. Again we are assured of the charity of God by His giving to us from His Spirit, and we bear witness (we, the apostles) to what we have seen, that God has once for all sent His Son to be saviour of the world. It is as if John gives here a recapitulation of his whole gospel; this section of the letter is not concerned with practical advice or exhortation as so much else of it is.

The *Jewish* apostles (the word is actually used for them by Eusebius and others, e.g. Eusebius, in his commentary on Isai 18:1–2, defines them as those who convey encyclical writings from their rulers) are not to be taken as adequate types of the Christian apostles who followed them. The eagerness to dilate on the office of *Shaliach* that began with the publication of *The Apostolic Ministry* in 1946 has now died down, after years of controversy. It cannot be said that the Jewish office throws very much light on the Christian. We have seen

earlier that Justin looked on this Jewish apostolate as baneful to Christians and no early writer seems to have seized upon the parallel as at all significant. When the Fathers looked for a parallel or prototype for the apostles of the Church, they do not bother about this Jewish institution but look to the OT prophets, with this significant difference, as Macarius points out (PG 34:573) that the prophets were individual stars for the house of Israel while the apostles were as the sun for the whole universe.

The link of the sending of the apostles with the Resurrection in John is not fortuitous. As Chrysostom says: "The apostles had at the outset little to say about the virgin birth, but say very much about the resurrection, since there were types of it, even if not wholly like, in former times; whereas they do not straightway speak of the virgin birth, but no more does the Virgin herself, who in Lk 2:48 speaks of 'thy father and I'."

The idea of the saviour-from-heaven has been claimed by Bultmann as something borrowed by John from the Mandeans, but their writings, which had all the spice of novelty when Bultmann began to use them in 1925, are now much better situated in their context. He appeals to them 109 times in his commentary on John. Thanks chiefly to the work of Lady Drower it is now quite clear that the Mandeans were neither pre-Christian nor independent of Christian influences, and the case for using them as a means of demythologizing John is thereby lost. The Johannine insistence on the parallel between the Sender and the Sent in heaven and on earth is not Mandean; it is in essentials a datum of the Synoptics.

XXIV

The Personality of John

THAT the author is a Palestinian Jew is coming to
be admitted even by those who would in former
times have been content to remain quite agnostic
about the personality of the author. A new German
evangelical work, for instance, sums up to the effect
that the author of the fourth gospel was one who was
quite at home with the places, seasons, personalities and
occurrences of Our Lord's life. If one adds to this the
fact that the Qumran documents—as we have had
occasion to see on our way through—while not actually
quoted by John yet show in places that ideas were
circulating there which were not so far removed from
John's, it then becomes necessary to admit that this
gospel, written as all admit so much later than the
others, goes back to a time when Jesus was still alive
for its ideas and local colour.

On the side of topography the gospel starts well with
(1:28) the locality given where John was baptizing and
then it continues with the events of the first week of
Jesus's public life, marking off the days one by one
until the miracle at Cana is reached (which must have
taken place on a Sunday since (2:1) the author skips
a day in his catalogue, presumably leaving out the
Sabbath). In this part of the gospel there is some
attempt to interpret Hebrew names, Rabbi, Messias,
Kephas, but it does not last. When we come to Aenon
near Salim (3:23) no attempt is made to give a translation of the Hebrew names. Sychar (4:5) is likewise

left alone, though its locality is obviously well known to the writer, but at the pool of Bethsaitha (5:2) he does give an interpretation. In the story of the multiplication of the loaves he keeps to the Palestinian point of view throughout by calling the lake "sea of Galilee" after the manner of Matthew and Mark,[1] though a word is added: "Galilee, which is Tiberias" (6:1). One can almost fancy the author thinking that his Western readers would have heard of Tiberias, but might not know about Galilee.

The well near Sychar is the deepest in Palestine. From its side one can see Mount Gerizim looking up in the background, the mountain on which the Samaritans still carry out their rites, and to the South the plain white for the harvest. How could an Asiatic Jew know all this if he had not had a Palestinian upbringing? The Jerusalem localities are equally well known to him; Gabbatha (= up there), where the governor had his paved court; the Skull-place, Golgotha; the two gardens; the brook Kedron, which is not mentioned by the Synoptics; the pool of Siloe, with its pregnant meaning; all these are familiar to the author, who, as we know from his first Epistle, was one who appreciated what men see and touch and handle with their hands (1 Jn 1:1). The feeding of the 5,000 is the only miracle related by all four gospels and the variants in John are indicative of his personality. He has left out all indication of the time of day, though (6:4) he adds that it was not far from the time of the Pasch; this dating of the event is significant in John, for it tells that what is to follow has a typological bearing on the Pasch (when the manna ceased and the Israelites had their first bread

[1] It is significant that Luke, who knew much bigger seas, never uses this word for the lake.

from the grain of the Promised land: Josue 5:11). Philip is named by John as the one who is "tempted" by Our Lord with His question about finding bread. The Synoptics have the apostles putting the question to Our Lord, but it is quite in His manner to turn it back on one of them, and Philip was known to some of the first audience of John, since he had worked in Asia. It was fitting therefore to introduce the small detail of his temptation. Andrew, who is named by John as producing the boy with the loaves, was also known in Asia Minor, and his practical sense, shown by his asking: "What is that among so many?" would be understood there. Mark has mentioned the 200 pence and the green grass, but it is John who recalls the abundance of grass, which would soon be burnt up in the heat of that depression, so many feet below sea-level. It is John, too, whose phrase (6:1 and 6:17) "across the sea" so clearly expresses what Matthew and Mark leave quite vague, that from the site of the feeding (located by the Byzantine mosaics at Tabgha) to Capharnaum one does *cross* the sea, or rather a wide bay which is formed by the lake at this NE end. No one who has stood at Tabgha and looked across would question the justice of the phrase. A final addition by John to the story is the command to gather up fragments, "that nothing be lost". The fact of gathering up is noted in the Synoptics and Mark has even added that they went round for the fish when they had filled twelve baskets with the broken bread. But why is this reason given for the gathering? It is easy to say that John is looking ahead to the Eucharist and has added this for liturgical reasons, but there is a quite sensible Jewish reason for the order. What was left over was normally the perquisite of the servers, and also (for a Jew) bread was too good to be

left about on a hillside. It was considered a profanation if animals found it and ate it. Further, if liturgy here predominates in John's mind, why does he go out of his way to speak of *barley* bread? There is no evidence that the early Church *insisted on* barley bread for the Eucharist. Barrett goes so far as to say that the command may be Jesus speaking symbolically of the gathering of the disciples, but that seems very wide of the mark.

One of John's favourite words is "freedom of speech" or παρρησία. He had it himself, as we are told (Ac 4:13 and 31), and the Synoptics speak of Jesus preaching the gospel with all freedom (only in Mk 8:32) a fact which John notes also (7:26 and 18:20). But in his Epistle (1 Jn 3:21; 4:17 and 5:14) it is something which the true Christian has for himself. One can see how much this would appeal to the former "Son of Thunder" who has not yet become a burnt out case. (We know he had not from Apoc on Babylon.) It is defined as the right to have granted us whatever we ask that is according to the will of God (i.e. security of petitioning).[1] This freedom of speech, we learn from 1 Jn 4:17, gives us confidence in the day of Judgment. "This is the perfection of *agape* amongst us that we have freedom of speech in the day of Judgment. For just as *He* is in the world, so are we also." It has been debated whether John refers to Christ or to the Holy Spirit here. The Spirit is the One who will judge (16:8), but the framing of the sentence makes it look like a reminiscence of 20:21: "Just as the Father has sent Me, so I also send you." As so often in Trinitarian matters, one cannot quite be sure to which Person John refers. 1 Jn 3:21 puts

[1] Note that *Alexandrinus* has brought this passage into line with Jn 14:13–14, but this is the less likely reading.

another condition for this freedom of speech: "If our heart does not accuse us." For then we should not be according to His will in our asking and in our use of the freedom. The tranquillity of the "abiding in Christ" that John so often speaks about is a strange contrast with the fiery quality of the Son of Thunder.

It was sufficiently established in the chapter on witnessing that in using the first person plural "We", John is speaking for the college of the apostles, of whom he is the last survivor. He keeps to this style in the opening of 1 Jn 1:1–4, though immediately he goes on (verse 7) to identify himself (and the apostles by implication) with the Christian community to whom he is writing. It is only in 3 Jn that *I* and *We* become distinct, as Hoskyns has so wisely noted. "I have written somewhat to the Church. But Diotrephes who loveth the first place there receiveth us not (i.e. *us*, the apostolic Church). Therefore, should I come, I will recall the works which he doth, prating of us with evil words." (3 Jn 9–10). It is not possible to say that when John speaks of the Word made flesh dwelling amongst us and adds: "We saw His glory", he means simply the Church in general. He must refer to the apostles only, for they saw His glory, some of them at the Transfiguration and all of them at the Ascension. The rest of the Church did not.

The last problem that remains is that of the possibility of John in the course of his long meditations having transformed the words of Jesus out of all recognition. From time to time in these chapters we have seen instances where that could not be true, where the agreement with the Synoptics was such that no transformation was possible. The more general objection that can be put on the score of the form in which the words are presented must now be considered. It is sometimes said

that the discourses of Jesus in John are poetical while in the Synoptics they are in prose. Jewish poetry was not a matter of counting feet in a strict quantitative scheme, but more like a Piers Plowman verse, with two stress accents in each half of the line and with other helps such as assonance and parallel constructions. Would Jesus have spoken in this elaborate way? And yet the discourse of Jn 6 at Capharnaum can be put back into just such a piece of Aramaic poetry, and this has been done. First it must be allowed that Jesus could have done it. The name that was foreshadowed for Him: "He shall be called *Nazoraios*" (Mt 2:23) does not mean that He shall be designated as the man from Nazareth; that would require *Nazarenos*. Rather it could mean that He shall be called the chanter or reciter of verse, as the late Rabbi Zolli once argued. If that were so, it may be that Jesus did on occasion speak in this simple verse-structure. It is not unwonted for men of the OT to lift up their voices in canticles and other verse-utterances. In the Synoptics the *Our Father* has this form, but for the most part they are reporting short interchanges of Jesus with his audience.

The claim of Bultmann to find the hand of an editor in the discourses of John is not very convincing.[1] He urges that the poetic form of the Prologue is broken by a lapse into prose at 1:6–8 and again at 1:15, and that these are editorial breaks. But the same kind of proceeding may be found in the eucharistic discourse at 6:28 and 6:41–42, and Fr. Gächter, when he analysed the poetic structure of that discourse, took these interruptions to be essential to mark the division of separate

[1] Dodd, in his *Historical Tradition in the Fourth Gospel*, p. 55, recognizes that in the Farewell Discourse, "the evangelist still had before his mind the common scheme of the Passion narrative."

strophes in the discourse. The psalms have to secure this by using the word *diapsalma* from time to time, but the insertion of a prose line would have the same effect.[1]

To start out with the assumption that John can never be found simply echoing the Synoptics, as Bultmann does, certainly makes it possible to argue at a later stage that where in fact Synoptic echoes are found in John, the hand of an editor may be detected seeking to harmonize this gospel with those the Church had long possessed, but the argument is no better than a logical circle, unless the initial assumption can be established independently, and this is not done. Synoptic sayings may be noted at 1:22; 1:32; 7:20; 11:2, and the reference (3:24) to the imprisonment of John the Baptist recalls what the Synoptics make a fixed point in their chronology, in so far as they have any. But in the course of this work there have been plenty of other echoes of the Synoptics noted, and that in matters of high doctrine as well as of local detail. One does not wish to devaluate the gospel of John by returning to the old view that it was written as a supplement to the Synoptics, but one cannot prescind from them when reading John. The knowledge of Mark shown in John has always been admitted, and not long ago Professor Kilpatrick argued cogently that John could be found to have quoted Matthew; the parallel of the Passion-narrative between Luke and John, along with the presence of some Johannine material in Luke has more recently come to be appreciated by many scholars.

[1] Fr. Alonso-Schökel has ample evidence of the alternation of poetry and prose in the Prophets; cf. the third section of his *Poetica Hebrea*.

Index of Scripture Passages

INDEX OF SCRIPTURE PASSAGES

157

INDEX OF SCRIPTURE PASSAGES

THE THEOLOGY OF ST. JOHN